SOCIALIST HISTORY

SOCIALIST HISTORY
OCCASIONAL PAPERS SERIES
No 21

LOCAL HISTORY SINCE 1945
ENGLAND, WALES, IRELAND

LIONEL MUNBY
D HUW OWEN
JAMES SCANNELL

2005

Published by the Socialist History Society, 2005

ISBN 0 9537742 8 7

Typeset by SHS, 2005.
www.socialisthistorysociety.co.uk

Contents

Foreword	2
Lionel Munby:	
Local History Studies in England	3
D Huw Owen:	
Local History Studies in Wales	30
James Scannell:	
Local History in the Republic of Ireland	42

Foreword

Some time ago the Socialist History Society committee expressed the view that it had been many years since the society, or its predecessor, had given attention the subject of local history, an area of study which has grown tremendously since the Second World War. It is an area of study, too, which connects to university adult education referred to by Lionel Munby in his article, and which, as the chairman of the Society for the Study of Labour History has recently written, has been virtually dismantled. This pamphlet is the outcome of that concern.

Initially, we intended to deal with developments in England alone but then decided to widen our approach to include Wales, Ireland and Scotland. Unfortunately it has not been possible to obtain a contribution about the local history situation in the last country, an omission we hope to rectify in any subsequent edition.

We have been fortunate, however, in being able to give a picture of what has happened elsewhere. Our contributors have a wide range of experience in writing about aspects of local history.

LIONEL MUNBY writes from his experience of the local history scene in Hertfordshire and for nearly forty years as Extra-Mural Staff Tutor at Cambridge University. From 1955 to 1975 he was editor of the *Local Historian*, journal of the British Association of Local History, and is the author of many books and articles. D HUW OWEN was Keeper of Pictures and Maps, National Library of Wales, Aberystwyth, and JAMES SCANNELL, a regular contributor to *Local History News* (BALH), is heavily involved in local history societies in Ireland.

We wish to thank them, and any who typed their contributions, for their generous co-operation, and to close in the traditional manner by saying that any errors and omissions are ours.

Chairman – A D Atienza
News Letter Editor – E H Dare.

Local History Studies in England

Lionel Munby

Before the Second World War: tentative beginnings
The writing of local history is of long standing, but the popular study of it has been transformed since the Second World War. Carew's *Survey of Cornwall* was published in 1602, Dugdale's *Antiquities of Warwickshire* in 1656. In the 1640s histories of Canterbury, Stamford, and Newcastle were published. Richard Gough's extraordinary parish history, *The Antiquities and Memoirs of Myddle* was written between 1700 and 1706, though not printed until the nineteenth century. During that century most English counties acquired antiquarian societies. In 1879 J C Cox published *How to Write the History of a Parish* and in 1898 C T Martin produced *The Record Interpreter*, described as 'really an amplification of the Appendix to the ninth edition of Wright's *Court Hand Restored* which I brought out in 1879'.[1] All these early local histories were, as W G Hoskins pointed out, the work of gentry and parsons and reflected their interests in manorial and ecclesiastical history. This approach to writing local history continued through the first half of the twentieth century. It was faithfully followed in the early *Victoria Histories of the Counties of England*, the first volume of which, *Hampshire Volume 1*, appeared in 1900.

In 1949 Osbert Lancaster produced his witty and brilliantly illustrated parody of this kind of history, *Draynflete Revealed*, the story of its development from village to city, a pointed and highly amusing take-off. The Fidget or ffigett family boasted 'a larger connection with the town than any other'[2] from Humfrey whose brass lies in the south aisle, the most prominent local citizen by the mid fifteenth century, to Miss Shelmerdine Parsley-Ffidgett who married four times and died in 1935 in a bathing accident. In the eighteenth century a much altered Draynflete was dominated by the Viscounts Littlehampton and Dr Palinure, celebrated Bishop of Horizon and the Isles. By the twentieth century the visitor went round the Museum and Art Gallery with a magnificent collection of Ffidget portraits and paced the bank of the 'limpid Drayne'.

When history became a respectable university subject in the nineteenth century, academics had no interest in any kind of local history. Their concern was with the history of the nation state. By the last quarter of the twentieth century a great deal of academic history, research themes and publication, was focussed on localities. This change had come about because of the growth of popular interest in local history, mainly in the third quarter of the century. How this happened is the theme of this study. The history of the local and particular became popular. This was history from below, of the common people, and entailed the use of source material. There were many obstacles to be overcome.

It is, perhaps, difficult for readers in the twenty-first century fully to appreciate the narrow-minded stuffiness of much history teaching in the universities and schools during the first half of the last century. While the content of university teaching was still centred on the nation state, economic history had gained a place, but not social history, least of all the history of the common people, history from below. Trevelyan's *English Social History* published in 1944 was rather frowned on by academics and in any case was described by an agricultural historian, who approved of it, as giving a 'yeoman's eye view of history' - and this did *not* quite mean Hoskins' *Midland Peasant* (1957). As for teaching methods, the student attended lectures but could not ask questions - never mind take part in discussions. Graduates may have had seminars, and at Oxbridge there were one-to-one tutorials to discuss an essay. Research was only for graduates, and they were usually flung into the water to learn to swim by dog-paddling. Until well after the Second World War university first degree history courses were based almost exclusively on secondary sources. There was little introduction to the primary evidence from which the conclusions which were to be questioned came. When documents were studied they were almost always in print. This was not only true of a 'special subject' like mine in early trade union history but also of Tudor and medieval topics. Many years after 1945, when Professor Elton wanted his Cambridge graduate students to learn how to read original Tudor documents, he had to send them to palaeography courses organised by the Board of Extramural Studies for their adult students. Only several years later did the history faculty organise its own palaeography classes for internal students. It is hardly surprising that when I began teaching local history I had never seen a manuscript, never mind learnt how to read earlier hands. Because I was a modern historian I had had no contact with Latin since taking School Certificate at fifteen.

In 1961 Dom David Knowles, then Regius Professor of Modern History at Cambridge University, was defending the current undergraduate syllabus from Peter Laslett's criticism of its 'refusal to recognise that what has happened since 1914 is also history'. Knowles countered with the argument that 'the acquisition of the historical sense ... to be nurtured must be fed by contact with segments of history that lend themselves to a long process of discovery and dialectic, and have been subjected to this treatment by historians of worth'. In plainer English this bluntly meant that the student should be reading the secondary sources in which older academics were arguing about old controversies and not waste their time trying to learn history from original sources. No wonder Laslett could point out that while 'the Russian Revolution of 1917 is that historical subject above all others about which every undergraduate must know something, no holder of a teaching post feels qualified to teach about this subject from the original documents'.[3]

The content of school teaching, at least up to the Second World War, tended to follow the pattern of kings, queens, generals, admirals, statesmen, battles and acts of parliament with the occasional disconnected insertion of dramatic events, such as the peasants' revolt, the reformation, the civil war, the industrial revolution, and the building of empire. Such history was amusingly parodied in 1930 by Sellars and Yeatman, in *1066 and All That*, which was dedicated 'to the Great British People without whose self-sacrificing determination to become top Nation there would have been no (memorable) history'.

'...Barons compelled John to sign the Magna Charter, which said:-

1. That no one was to be put to death, save for some reason - (except the Common People).

2. That everyone should be free - (except the Common People)...

Magna Charter was therefore the chief cause of Democracy in England, and thus a *Good Thing* for everyone (except the Common People).'[4]

This limited view of history was, of course, challenged by Sidney and Beatrice Webb's *History of Trade Unionism* (1894 and 1920), and G D H Cole's many publications, from *The World of Labour* (1913) onwards. These works uncovered the wealth of institutions created by working people, but they tended to treat this in isolation as a thing on its own. It was not really until Cole and Postgate's *The Common People* of 1938 that the impact of working people on general history was properly discussed, but even then only in the context of an industrialised society. In 1938 A L Morton's *A People's History of England* challenged the basic philosophy of the traditional history establishment from a Marxist point of view, but Morton did not write history from below in any new sense; his theme was still the nation.

It was only after the Second World War that local history really took off and began to influence the interpretation of all of English history. It is in some ways surprising that this was in the field of rural, not industrial or urban history. The reason, of course, was because the creative influence was W G Hoskins and his interest and prejudices for long were dominant.

Hoskins did not start from scratch. Branches of the Historical Association were producing local bibliographies before the First World War. In 1925 it formed a Village History Committee which in 1928-29 became the Local History Committee and produced a simple bibliography of local history.[5] The National Council of Social Service began publishing a series of Local History Leaflets in 1938 through its Local History Sub-Committee, which became the Standing Conference for Local History in 1948. Leaflet No 1 opens: 'Recently there has been a remarkable growth of interest on the part of village groups and individuals in the possibilities of local history as a subject of study and practical work ... it is only recently that local history has been approached from a different angle [to the traditional antiquarian one] as a subject for study, research and record by groups of village people not necessarily equipped with special knowledge or training'.[6] Many of these helps and aids for non-academic students of local history published before the Second World War, especially those by the Historical Association, were directed at schools. There were astonishing achievements such as the remarkable book on the tiny village of Hexton in north Hertfordshire, privately printed and published in 1936. This two hundred page 'Parish Survey' made and compiled by the senior scholars of the Herts. C.C. School' was completed and 'edited by Ralph J Whiteman (Headmaster)'.

There were parallel early developments among adult educationalists. The unconfirmed minutes of a conference of tutors held at the University of Leeds on 4 January 1913 under the auspices of the Central Joint Advisory Council on Tutorial Classes contain the following passages: 'reported on the work being done in connection with the Manchester Classes. - A syllabus for research work had been drawn up and four centres were engaged in investigating the life of a town (its Municipal organisation, trade union activities, etc). Help was also given in regard to private study and reading.' 'A letter was read advocating the producing of some piece of co-operative work in the nature of a class thesis'. 'The Chairman (R H Tawney) reported that one of his students in Staffordshire was going to try to produce a book on work and life in the Potteries, and urged that there was a great field before the classes in the presentation of working class problems from a working class point of view.'[7] Though Tawney's 1913 advice and example does not seem to have been followed between the world wars, there was local history teaching in adult classes. Fred Brooks always claimed that he was the first regular local history tutor, working for what was then the University College of Hull, and that this teaching played an important part in developing popular support, locally, for the University. In Cambridge, W P Baker was taking extramural classes in village history from 1934. He was a real village historian who, among other things, founded a local Cottage Improvement Society.

It would be a mistake to think that all of the new interest in 'the history of the village itself', to quote Hoskins, which developed in the early twentieth century took place in educational institutions. There were remarkable individuals who had a 'conversion'. One such was the Rev Andrew Clark, who wrote to an acquaintance on 6 December 1913: 'When I came here, 20 years ago, I had much writing to do about Oxford University and its Colleges, about the extraordinary language of the Basques, and about Monasteries and their records. I would have been much better employed, had I set to, at once, to search out the remarkable history of this most interesting parish.' It is no accident that this parson kept superb diaries recording local events in the First World War.[8]

The difficulties to be overcome

It was only after the Second World War that local history really took off, and history from below began to influence the interpretation of all of English history. An early example of the change is S G Thicknesse's *Abbots Langley* of 1946 which opened with the words: 'Once upon a time, historians foolishly imagined that only kings and wars and the jury system were history; but now we know that history is made not less by the countless thousands of ordinary people'.[9] The major influence in making the change was W G Hoskins, whose first popular work, in 1949, made clear a new approach. This was *Midland England* in which a chapter on 'The Old Midland Village' described 'ordinary men and women, and the old village in which they lived out their sober and quiet lives. I have read many hundreds of manuscript inventories of Midland villagers attached to their old wills'.[10] Hoskins was to play a major part in making the study of local history popular with non-professionals. Individuals and groups in adult education classes and working on their own became expert local historians.

This was not easy in the early days. There were many obstacles and practical difficulties. Most of what the local historian in the twenty-first century takes for granted did not exist in the 1940s. Not only were there no computers and no word processors, but there was no photocopying. There were few county record offices and those that did exist had minimal, cramped search room facilities. There were very few books in print on sources or methods and the specialised societies which have proliferated since did not exist. For example at Hertfordshire, which had long been accumulating records, the search room was the county archivist's fairly small office. The archivist sat at one table with his secretary; researchers, two or three at the most, sat at another table. There were bonuses. In Hertfordshire I could visit the basement storage rooms, penetrate the upstairs store room safe, and poke about on my own. Students in adult classes, however, could only have typescript copies, produced on old-fashioned Gestetner duplicating machines, of someone else's transcript. There was no opportunity until photocopying spread for an adult education class to learn and practise palaeography on local documents.

Because county record offices were few and inadequately equipped, the archives which the local historian needs to study were to a great extent scattered in many different places, from the family libraries, or cellars even, of county families, to lawyers' safes, to local government offices, in parish church chests, almost anywhere in fact. Research entailed detective work as to the whereabouts of sources as well as in their interpretation. There were compensations, sometimes exciting if not always comfortable. Some of my own experiences may suggest what it was like. I came across two Tithe Awards in disconcerting situations. Let loose in the vestry of Harpenden's church one cold winter evening - and the vestry was bitterly cold - I kicked the old fashioned large pipe central heating under the table in trying to warm my feet. Alarmingly a considerable section of piping seemed to come away and roll towards me. It was in fact a metal tube which turned out to contain the Tithe Award, which no one knew was there. On another occasion in the equally cold vestry of Hemel Hempstead church, working with a group of adult students, someone said, 'I wonder where that trapdoor in the roof leads to.' Naturally we climbed up to find out. The substantial roof space looked like the set for a Hammer ghost film, festooned with enormous trailers of cobwebs. Hanging from a beam in the midst of this was a huge roll, which, when unrolled, proved to be Hemel Hempstead's Tithe Award.

While the relevant historical records, the basic sources for the local historian, were so inaccessible, there was not much even in print to guide the beginner. The only available books on sources in 1949 were the Orwins' *Open Fields* (1938), Cheney's *Handbook of Dates* (1945), Tate's *Parish Chest* (1946), and a Historical Association *English Local History Handlist* (1947). C T Martin's *Record Interpreter* was reprinted in 1949. What was entirely missing, however, were books on 'how to do it'. Tate's *Parish Chest* was, however, a goldmine. It described 'the principal classes of records available for the use of the parish historian, and should give him some help in interpreting these records'.[11]

There were other obstacles to the popular study of local history in the years just after the Second World War. Not only was the *Parish Chest* unique as an aid to amateur research but the very idea of amateurs doing it was anathema to academics. When I used the word 'research' in connection with a university tutorial class as late as the 1960s I was told in no uncertain terms by the academic members of my Board that 'in Cambridge the word research is only used for PhD work'.[12] A measure of the change which has occurred is that in 1979 I was asked to prepare a paper for the Universities Council for Adult Education annual conference on 'the planning and organisation of research-based courses in local history'.

What local historians were interested in seemed trivia to academics whose thoughts were still focused on the nation state. There was an old and lasting prejudice against recording the minutiae from which the local history of ordinary people and ordinary places must be built. This was at the best 'antiquarianism', an emotive word. There is an amusing handwritten nineteenth century comment on an index in the Hertford County Record Office which reveals how wide the gulf was. It is added to the manuscript index to the Archdeaconry of Huntingdon's 'Admon Bds., Inventories, Accounts, etc.' which are described as containing 'dusty trifles, the personal touches in which are as the fragments of dead moths and remnants of cocoons found sometimes among long neglected clothes'. The index in which this comment occurs was 'copied from slips made by the late Ernest Cheyne in 1888'. It continued: 'Uncalled-for criticism:- The enthralling interest of these entries is almost too much for the ordinary human being. It is witness to the marvels of nature, that there are human creatures to whom the sound or sight of "Ad.Bd.Inv." gives more pleasure than Shelley's "Skylark". I really can't understand how Ernest Cheyne, a man of the highest intelligence and most clear profound sincerity, could have laboured so assiduously in such dusty trifles ... did his romantic energy truly run in these curious channels - the Houndsditches of history? I cease baffled ... I incline to think he verily liked the work'.[13]

The local historian's answer was given by a young undergraduate in an issue of *The Amateur Historian*. 'There is an urge within local communities to find out detail and fact about the past life of the village - people want to know the history of a certain chair, or who donated the stained glass windows, or the day, month and year when the manor house was burnt down - the study of events *per se* has always been a satisfying art.'[14] I would add that a growing body of local people wanted to know why as well as when, to understand the significance of events.

The historians who made local history popular and accessible

A sea change began in the 1950s. Five full-time historians were, in particular, the inspiration. Thanks to them and a group of tutors in adult education the study of local history became a popular activity. An indication of this came when a full 'history' of the fictional radio village of Ambridge was published. In the process of popularisation the boundaries of historical research were widened. Three of the five pioneering historians were associated with the Department of English Local History opened in the University of Leicester in 1948. W G Hoskins was its first head; H P R Finberg succeeded him as Reader in 1951 when Hoskins went to Oxford as Reader in Economic History. Finberg became a Professor in 1964, retiring in 1965 when Hoskins left Oxford to succeed him as Professor. He was replaced at Oxford by Joan Thirsk who came from the Leicester department. Hoskins retired in 1968, Joan Thirsk in 1983. These three opened the whole world of pre-industrial rural England and its records to the non-academic reader. Maurice Beresford, from Leeds University, was a fourth university teacher; his research covered a wider area. The fifth was W E Tate whose *Parish Chest* has been mentioned.

Outlines of what each of these historians did will explain how they changed the study of English history.

W E Tate was a village schoolmaster and WEA tutor who, as a mature student, became an Oxford B.Litt. He had a remarkable capacity to accumulate information. The *Parish Chest* reveals this. In 1967 he published The *English Village Community and the Enclosure Movements*. This arose from what had been a major interest since 1930. Tate died in 1968. He had 'spent the last thirty years of his life in tracing and classifying enclosure acts and awards for every English county. By 1968, he had published "handlists" for twenty seven counties and had assembled information on many more. Despite unwearying industry and devotion, Tate's work remained unfinished at his death.' In 1978 the University of Reading published *A Domesday of English Enclosure Acts and Awards*, which gathered together Tate's handlists and included 'acts and awards of which he was not aware'.[15] This enormous book, of 460 8" x 11½" pages, is an appropriate tribute to Tate's energy. In conversation during a radio broadcast in 1964 Tate made a valid point which illustrates the value of local history. 'Many of the enclosure historians have never seen an enclosure award or act, and the result is that a good deal of their work isn't worth the paper it's written on.' While not going quite so far, I have met teachers who admitted that only after seeing an enclosure award had they really understood the historical controversies about enclosure.[16]

W G Hoskins was an Exeter man, a Devonian who became the doyen of the 'Leicester School'. The nine books which he published between 1951 and 1959, an extraordinarily productive decade, reveal how his writing inspired and encouraged many individuals and students in adult education classes to research and write about the localities in which they lived.[17] Of these nine, three are especially important, *The Making of the English Landscape* became a classic. It inaugurated a major series of county landscape histories, edited by Hoskins, to which Finberg contributed *Gloucestershire* in 1955 and Hoskins himself *Leicestershire* in 1957. *The Midland Peasant* was Hoskins' major historical work and, revealingly, was dedicated 'to R H Tawney as a grateful tribute'. *Local History in England* was 'a book of advice and encouragement for local historians in any part of England' as Hoskins described it in his Preface. A reviewer described it as 'written in an unassuming, almost conversational style ... the book contains an enormous amount of information and yet never makes the reader feel that he is being crammed with facts'.[18] Hoskins was such an outstanding influence partly because he wrote so well and directly for beginners and non-academic local historians but also because the historical period of which he wrote and the documentary sources for studying it were relatively easy to tackle. Hoskins was an old fashioned Liberal with a conscience. He was elected to the local council when he returned to his native Exeter. When he discovered the misdeeds of the hereditary clique who had controlled the city for decades he criticised them publicly and had to pay £1000 after a subsequent libel action. It was said that he has taken the historian's revenge, leaving a substantial 'Black Book' for future publication.

H P R Finberg was another West Country man, a printer by trade who became a full time historian later in life, but he proved immensely productive.[19] He created a major stir in 1955 with *Roman and Saxon Withington: a study in continuity*, in which he argued from topographical and documentary evidence the then heretical proposition that there had been continuity of settlement from Roman to Saxon times. In 1962 I had the privilege of interviewing Finberg on the BBC about this. 'Dr Finberg, what were you trying to do at Withington?'

'I wanted to test the idea that the coming of the Anglo-Saxons involved a complete break in the life of British villages. For many years we've been told that the end of Roman rule was a catastrophe that left a clear slate on which the English proceeded to draw their own pattern; to me that's just incredible.'

'How did you set about this?'

'I set about mastering the topography of the parish in the first place, In the course of a good many visits I walked over the length and breadth of it. And of course I had long talks with the local people - especially the farmers. Then I read the archaeological record, such as it was. And lastly I studied the documents which were, as I expected, plentiful.' This is a model of how to set about a study of local topographical history. Finberg went on to explain that he was able 'to reconstruct the ancient pattern of the parish - its trackways and roads and the layout of its fields'. 'The place came through the twilight between the Roman and Saxon periods with its boundaries more or less intact ... as a going concern ... probably run mainly as a sheep farm in the Roman period ... when the English got there they used it at first in that way. In the period after Domesday there was much more corn growing.'

When asked 'how you traced boundaries', Finberg answered: 'An Anglo-Saxon description of the boundary takes you round about 15 miles of the country, and what I did was to walk over it'.

'Could you identify on the ground place after place in the Anglo-Saxon description?'

'Oh yes'.[20]

It was Finberg who described what became known as the Leicester view of the nature of local history. This was 'to portray for readers, the Origin, Growth, Decline, and Fall of a Local Community'. He defined a community as 'a set of people occupying an area with defined territorial limits and so far united in thought and action as to feel a sense of belonging together, in contradistinction from the many outsiders who do not belong. This definition obviously fits the national community. It also fits, or has fitted in the past, many a smaller social aggregate, both rural and urban ... In the local, the national, and the supra-national community we have three distinct manifestations of social life ... three distinct fields of study for the historian.'[21] Finberg played a more active part than Hoskins in public organisations which helped the amateur historian. He was for many years a most positive influence in the committee work of the Standing Conference for Local History.

Joan Thirsk was a worthy successor to Hoskins and Finberg. She came from the same Leicester department and she took over from Hoskins as Reader in Economic History at Oxford in 1965, retiring in 1983. She did not, like them, write of what local history was, nor of how to study it. She was an agricultural historian, but one for whom the locality was all-important. She wrote, in 1999, that she had 'found my central interest in agricultural history, and particularly in the study of local differences, rather than in the more conventional task of lumping all differences together to make a set of large generalities'.[22] So she was happy to serve as an officer of the British Association for Local History and supported local historians all her working life: 'my interest in analysing the distinctive characteristics and personalities of farming regions, and in exploring the interaction of those regions on each other, has persisted and deepened over the years, being always mixed with a desire to bring historic scenes to life by actual examples from the doings and writings of identifiable people'.[23]

Joan Thirsk was a prolific writer and editor on the widest range of subjects related to agrarian history.[24] R H Tawney had been her supervisor and 'his writing left an indelible impression' on her.[25] He wrote an introduction to her early work, *Fenland Farming* in which he described England as 'a country in which an unusual diversity of soils and land configuration are packed into a small compass. Her agriculture and the societies based upon it have been equally diverse'. This might have been the text for a description of Joan Thirsk's work.[26] Her *Economic Policy and Projects* of 1978 'transformed our view of the economy and the process of growth in the sixteenth and seventeenth centuries'.[27] Joan Thirsk commented, revealingly, in 1999 that 'economic history would never have captivated me, as it did, if I had been introduced to it in its present-day guise, dominated by the need to count anonymous heads and manipulate mathematical equations'. She described the influence on her thinking of 'being educated wholly by women [who seek] to study people and situate them in their immediate geographical and intellectual circle, while men favour trends in government, politics, religion, and the economy'.[28]

M W Beresford from Leeds University was a pioneer, along with J G Hurst, in the study of deserted medieval villages (DMVs). Together they carried out the first major excavation, of Wharram Percy. His *Lost Villages* of 1954 was followed by local studies in the Leicester series of 'Occasional Papers'.[29] This led him into a broad and fascinating exposition of field work. *History on the Ground* described six journeys. One was 'among deserted villages', another was 'along boundaries' in which he described how to trace a parish boundary as Finberg had done at Withington. Beresford explained that 'much of the incentive to carry out local investigations came from work undertaken in collaboration with Dr J K St Joseph'.[30] Their collaboration led to the publication in the next year, 1958, of *Medieval England: an aerial survey*, which was to make aerial photography into a major source for understanding the history of the landscape.

Beresford ranged widely in landscape history. In 1967 he published his monumental *New Towns of the Middle Ages*. He had been, he wrote, 'seduced from agricultural history by reading T F Tout's essay "Medieval Town Planning", while considering subjects for the anthology of air photographs which Dr J K St Joseph and I published'. Beresford's interests were wide. In a BBC interview in 1964 he described how 'a group of students in Leeds have been looking at what is now slum property and working out the ratio of servants to members of the family which is very high ... even back to back houses with attics could run to one or two servants', a revealing insight into Victorian society. In the same broadcast he gave valuable advice: 'amateurs faced with a formidable mass of documents can, without being at all immoral, have recourse to sampling. Another technique which I've sometimes used myself is to work backwards. If you start at the beginning on a completely strange matter it's often difficult to see what it's all about. If you get the final decision after some long controversy, irrelevant things have been dropped. Working one's way backwards is as good a way for amateurs to get into things as to start at the beginning.'31

Margaret Spufford applied the ideas of these historians to new aspects of local history in the county of Cambridge in the sixteenth and seventeenth centuries. She wrote 'The Schooling of the Peasantry in Cambridgeshire 1575-1700' for the Finberg festschrift edited by Joan Thirsk; this was a study of peasant literacy and inheritance patterns and of the dissenting laity. It was reproduced in Part 2 of her *Contrasting Communities* of 1974, a major exploration of Cambridgeshire local history. In Part 1 she compared the social structure, land distribution, inheritance customs, and provision for women in three different villages, Chippenham, Orwell and Willingham. While small holdings survived in a fenland village like Willingham, they did not in the upland villages. 'The engrossing movement and the "disappearance of the small landowner" accelerated' in the upland parishes. 'Parishioners and their Religion' in Part 3 was a remarkable study of the spread of dissent among the laity before and after the Commonwealth. 'Puritan religious convictions were, in this county, a grass-roots phenomenon amongst the very humble, which predated the Commonwealth ... The Family of Love flourished, in the 1570s, in areas where Quakerism was found in the 1650s ... We know that the ordinary villager had religious convictions of his own ... No single social background is common to all the communities which were deeply affected by dissent.' All these important conclusions were based on thorough research, which is the more impressive because Margaret Spufford with admirable, but unfortunately not so common, honesty confesses the limitations of her sources. In Part 1, 'surveys contain holdings which do not appear in court rolls. Court rolls contain transactions between tenants who are unnamed in surveys, and parish registers contain data which do not harmonise with either. Only the wills, once carefully analysed, give a feeling of reliability'. In Part 3 'the evidence for individual religious belief among the peasantry is thoroughly unsatisfactory, yet there is enough to show that the importance of the parish church and its rival, the meeting house, was very great to the layman'. 32

New publications and new specialist societies

The writings and broadcasts of these historians from the 1950s to the 1970s were only part of an explosion of new publications on local history.33 I believe Francis Celoria's *Teach Yourself Local History* of 1958 was the first really helpful book published, because it did not assume existing knowledge. Joscelyne Finberg's *Exploring Villages*, a stimulating exercise in what to look for, appeared in the same year. W G Hoskins' magisterial *Local History in England* did not appear until the next year, 1959. R B Pugh's *How to Write a Parish History* was an alarming turn-off for the non-academically educated, though it was and is admirable for the more experienced student who wishes to research to professional standards. 'The local historian must know Latin' (p. 12). 'The local historian must be able to read ... the several varieties of court hand practised in this country from the thirteenth century until 1731 and the "Secretary Hand".' (pp. 13-14). I have forgotten most of the classical Latin which I had learnt before I was fifteen and I have never tried to read court hands. I only learnt to read Secretary Hand properly in 1966, attending a residential course taken by F G Emmison. This does not mean that I never became a local historian, but that I have only researched and worked with students on original documents from the sixteenth century onwards. Precisely because I began working as a local historian with no expertise, because I had to 'muddle through', to learn by doing, it has been easier to understand the problems met by beginners and to help them.

Eileen Gooder's *Latin for Local Historians* was a godsend for many new local historians whose Latin, like mine, was either very rusty or non-existent. M W Barley's *The English Farmhouse and Cottage* was invaluable for those working with inventories. It revealed the plans and shapes, put walls and roofs on the theoretical houses abstracted from the documents and explained regional differences. John West's *Village Records* gave the beginner an exemplary introduction, with examples, to the main sources. David Dymond showed the beginner how to turn his researches into a readable and publishable form. His *Writing Local History* of 1981 was republished by the British Association of Local History in 1999 as *Researching and Writing History: a practical guide for local historians*. In this rewritten version 'the central purpose remains, as before, to investigate how we discipline ourselves to write better'. The opening section describes 'the present state of local history'; it is lucid, wide ranging and comprehensive.

As the quantity and, for the most part, the quality of published books on local history increased, so did the formation of new societies catering for specialised interests.[34] Three important new areas of study emerged: industrial archaeology in 1963 with Kenneth Hudson's book of that name; population history with the creation of the Cambridge Group by Peter Laslett, Tony Wrigley and Roger Schofield; and vernacular architecture inspired by the work of John Smith of the Royal Commission for Historical Monuments.

This expansion brought new information and new ideas, broadening the local historian's horizons, but the explosion caused problems. Alan Everitt, who became head of the Department of English Local History at Leicester in 1968 described them: 'It is no exaggeration to say that in recent years the study of English Local History has exploded in all directions. As we seek to practise it, moreover, it demands not only a working knowledge of the historical field as a whole, but a certain acquaintance with such related disciplines as historical geography, archaeology, anthropology, economic history, demography, folklore, English Literature, place-name studies, and vernacular architecture. While it is this that makes the subject an exciting intellectual challenge, and has occasioned many interdisciplinary seminars by outside speakers, it may eventually force us to modify our traditionally encyclopaedic approach, though in doing so we should be grievously impoverished'.[35]

I spoke about the problem in a talk in 1972: 'Everyone seems to want to found a new society and to publish a new journal, understandably from the point of view of the specialist, enthusiast. But what happens to the ordinary, "amateur", local historian, or even the so-called "professional" tutor? The specialist "know-how" that the all-round local historian seems to need grows all the time. Sometimes it seems trivial but it can be quite maddening if you are ignorant. How can you begin hedge-dating, if you can't identify shrubs? How can you use the evidence of buildings without the knowledge of building materials and building techniques? How can you use demographic evidence without some statistical knowledge? The fully professional recording of oral evidence requires not only knowledge of phonetics and a great deal of understanding of human beings, especially old people, but also technical equipment, a good tape recorder and know-how in its use. This is our dilemma: the local historian has to be an all-rounder, to an extent that the academic specialist has never imagined.' So the local historian had to work with others in a group. The possibilities were explored in Alan Rogers' *Group Projects in Local History* in 1977.

Adult education

It was through adult education that interest in local history spread, producing both readers and active amateur workers. University extramural and extension departments and the Workers Educational Association provided evening classes all over the country, in which people learnt how to find out about their own locality and began to write and publish local histories. The growth of new types of adult education classes in which students began working on source material themselves, realising the intentions of those pioneer tutors in 1913, was closely connected with the spread of local publications based on students' original work, and financed either by the students themselves or by WEA Districts and Extramural Departments. At first these tended to be pamphlets or booklets. Arthur Brown inspired the production of a great many such booklets for Essex villages from 1949 (13 between 1949 and 1959). These were usually brief, dealt only with the last two centuries and were often duplicated, but they were a remarkable enterprise. Dr Priestley began taking a London University Tutorial class in 1954 at Upminster. When the class finished in 1957 they set about publishing not one booklet, but six, and their sales paid for them all. Rex Russell began his marvellous series of studies of Lincolnshire enclosures with Nettleton in 1960 and Victor Skipp began his remarkable studies of parishes which were absorbed into Birmingham, with *Discovering Sheldon* about the same time (1960-61). All these publications were products of joint studies by members of adult classes led by tutors. My own such publications began in 1953. Ten places in Hertfordshire, and three in Cambridgeshire produced their own publications; in Kings Langley two were books.

In Czechoslovakia, in 1962, when invited to read a paper on teaching local history to adult students I received an unexpected compliment on our cooperative work. A young translator who had read my paper was interpreting for me the keynote Czech contribution. He whispered in my ear: 'It is ironic, Mr Munby, that in our socialist country our best teachers can only describe the work of individuals, while you from a capitalist country tell us how to organise collective work.'

The individuals who came to these classes continued studying on their own and founded new local history societies in their home areas, societies which unlike many older ones met in the evenings, not in the daytime. They were no longer the preserve of people of independent means and the retired but were often run by working people.

The most astonishing products of adult education classes in local history came from the extramural department of Leeds University and the WEA. These three monumental books (504, 492 and 520 pages respectively) were edited by adult tutors but essentially the work of adult students in tutorial classes in the Yorkshire dales.[36] It is no accident that from the same Leeds department's staff came in 1963 Edward Thompson's classic *The Making of the English Working Class*. Though this is national rather than local history, it 'was written in Yorkshire and is coloured at times by West Riding sources. I have learned a great deal from members of my tutorial classes, with whom I have discussed many of the themes treated'.[37] Edward Thompson's later explorations of eighteenth century history, after he moved to the University of Warwick, were of local incidents. His wife, Dorothy, wrote about local Chartist history.

There were, of course, many other able adult tutors doing research themselves and stimulating their students. Marion Springhall in Suffolk and Rachel Young in Norfolk both worked for Cambridge, Kenneth MacMahon and Edward Gillett for Hull.[38] Owen Ashmore at Manchester and Joe Bagley at Liverpool were early pioneers. The opening to public viewing of the mid-nineteenth century censuses under the hundred years rule was an opportunity for many local historians to work on the social structure of their communities. Peter Tillott of Sheffield University extramural department undertook many studies with local groups of adult students, for which he developed a simple system of analysis.

In May 1968 Alan Rogers of Nottingham University organised a conference of local history tutors in adult education at Matlock. The people whom this brought together had considerable achievements behind them and many more to come. They included Joe Bettey from Bristol who has written widely on west country history, Christopher Charlton whose work from the Tawney centre in Matlock inspired the work of many adult students in Derbyshire, Fred Lansberry from Oxford, later from Kent where he stimulated and produced local history, Bill Liddell from London, for some time a loner in his department, and Denis Stuart of Keele University who in 1992 published *Manorial Records* and in 1995 *Latin for Local and Family Historians*.

Out of this Matlock conference came a new organisation, a Conference of Local History Tutors which met annually. In April 1981 it became the Association of Local History Tutors which has flourished ever since. In May 2002 there were 84 members, five of whom had been at the 1968 first meeting.

The work of two adult tutors who were not at this conference in 1968 has been extremely important in the growth of local history since. John Morris of University College, London who was also a part-time adult education tutor for Cambridge and the first editor of *Past and Present*, produced for Phillimore a county-by-county translation of *Domesday Book*. Barrie Trinder, a Shropshire Education Committee adult tutor from 1965, shone a new light on the industrial revolution with his work on Coalbrookdale and Ironbridge.[39]

Historical organisations

The Historical Association, through its Local History Committee, has published useful pamphlets regularly. *The English Local History Handlist* of 1947, often reprinted and revised, has been an established tool for local historians. The association published Michael Rix's *Industrial Archaeology* in 1967 and, in their *Helps for Students of History* series, pamphlets on title deeds, smaller houses, local records in print, and reading archives of the sixteenth and seventeenth centuries. Most valuable have been the two series of 'Short Guides to Records', the first of which, edited by myself, were printed in *History* between 1961 and 1971 and as a booklet in 1972. The second series, edited by Kate Thompson, was published in 1993-94 and as a booklet in 1997.[40]

Alongside the new books and new societies formed in the third quarter of the twentieth century came the growth of new national organisations. The National Council for Social Services (NCSS) had a Local History Sub-Committee in the 1930s. It encouraged work by village groups, publishing *Local History Leaflet* No 1 in July 1938 with suggestions for how to organise local history work on a county basis. The Standing Conference for Local History (SCLH) grew out of this earlier sub-committee in 1948. Its executive brought together prominent academics and active field workers under the chairmanship of Philip Whitting of St Paul's School and a remarkable and tireless secretary, Bettie Miller. SCLH worked hard to create and support county committees. Local bodies, ranging from Women's Institutes to learned societies and educational organisations, were invited to a conference to create a coordinating body for the many different organisations involved. There was no intention to form new independent societies, though this did happen. There were real sources of conflicts from, for example, Norfolk whose existing antiquarian society believed it could do all that was necessary for its area, to an enthusiastic social service worker who told an SCLH annual conference that three named counties had no local history activity because they had no county committees. The editor of the county journal in one of the named counties pointed out that his society had a large and active membership and had been publishing for a century while SCLH had not yet reached its teens. A great deal of creative work was, however, carried out. The county local history committees in many English counties are standing memorials to the work of SCLH.

By 1977 local history had become such a widespread activity that an SCLH committee, with Lord Robert Blake as chairman and Dr Edward Miller as his deputy, reviewed the situation. The committee reported in 1979 emphasising the need for 'a national organisation concerned solely with the subject and its practitioners. The SCLH could serve as the foundation on which to build the agency we envisage.' A group of twelve people under the chairmanship of Dr Joan Thirsk was asked to consider 'the form in which the main objectives of an independent national body for local history might be expressed, and the organisational structure' best suited to fulfil them. They reported to the SCLH AGM and Conference on 19 September 1980. Eighteen months later, on 1 April 1982, this independent organisation, the British Association for Local History (BALH) came into being. This was a big leap, for BALH had no financial backing such as NCSS had given to SCLH. It had to raise money from individuals and institutions who had not paid for membership before, and from charitable foundations. The Gulbenkian supported much of the early publications. Until the summer of 1984 the NCVO (National Council of Voluntary Organisations), which NCSS had become, gave BALH office space and Bettie Miller served as administrative secretary. BALH took over those county local history committees which were agreeable and all SCLH's publications, including *The Local Historian.*

By March 1983 BALH had just over 1,200 paying members. There were turbulent meetings in the early days over the extent of regional representation on the governing body. Bettie Miller, as secretary in the early years, had to sort out the conflicts with the help of Norman McCord, the chairman. David Hayns was appointed as Field Officer for two years with a brief to 'travel throughout the country to cooperate in developing interest, work and projects in local history among individuals and groups'. In November 1983 he produced a most impressive 'report' of seventy A4 pages which gave a comprehensive picture of the immense amount of local history activity in the country. BALH went through several ups and downs but grew to become the effective national organisation of local historians. When Lt Col Michael Cowan became first administrator and later general secretary its efficiency, financial situation, and public image were immensely improved. I had the honour of being elected President from 1995 to 2000.

The Historians' Group of the Communist Party had a much smaller impact but it brought people to local history both as consumers and as producers. It stressed labour history, but not exclusively. Eric Hobsbawm has described its wider influence: 'There is little doubt that the rise of social history in Britain as a field of study, and especially of "history from below" or the "history of the common people", owes a great deal to the work of members of the group, e.g. Hilton, Hill, Rudé, E P Thompson, Hobsbawm, Raphael Samuel'.[41] From October 1950 the group published a duplicated monthly *Local History Bulletin* which described itself as 'bold enough to regard this as the forerunner of a printed magazine, however distant that may seem at the moment' In October 1953 the Bulletin was retitled *Our History*. From 1956 *Our History* was published as a series of pamphlets on single historical themes. In time it acquired a stiff cover and was produced by photolitho.

An *Our History Journal* commenced publication in 1977 with articles and reports on similar topics. These two publications added enormously to the historical understanding of labour history especially in particular local areas, but they hardly impinged on wider local history. The early Bulletin reported the work of local groups and gave advice on suitable topics and how to study them. While the emphasis was on the history of the working class movement, there was a great deal about English history in general. The retitled *Our History* had articles on subjects as varied as 'Humanising the Poor Law', 'The Railway Navvy', 'The Gloucestershire Weavers' Rising of 1756', 'Unemployed Marchers of Fifty Years Ago' with a follow-on called 'Boots'. The coverage of the pamphlets after 1956 was as wide. Among the first twelve issues were 'Luddism', 'Some Dilemmas for Marxists 1900-14', 'Enclosure and Population Change', 'Town Privileges and Politics in Tudor and Stuart England'. I edited Nos 29-54 and a volume of twelve of the essays which had been published between 1956 and 1968.[42] *Our History* continued publication until 1992 (No 87), shortly after the British Communist Party had dissolved. *Our History Journal* was succeeded in 1993 by the Socialist History Society's printed *Socialist History Journal* which deals, among other things, with labour history. *Our History* was succeeded by the SHS Occasional Papers series.

History Workshop: a journal of socialist historians was born in 1976 out of the History Workshops organised by Raphael Samuel at Ruskin College over the previous ten years. Samuel had been a member of the Communist Party Historians' Group.

Journals

The launching in 1952 of *The Amateur Historian*, which became *The Local Historian* in 1968, added greatly to the local historian's armoury. The founder and first editor was Terrick FitzHugh, who worked as a film producer but 'his real love and interest lay in local history and genealogy'; his *Dictionary of Genealogy* (1985, revised edition 1988) is outstandingly useful. As chairman of the Sunbury and Shepperton Local History Society he realised that 'there were no periodicals catering for the non specialist' and so he launched *The Amateur Historian*, a private venture and far from secure financially. He was not rich and certainly he could not have financed the running of a journal on a permanent basis, but he did finance the effective launch of a publication paying a tiny royalty. It was FitzHugh who laid down and followed the principles which guided the editorial policy of the journal for many decades. He wrote in his first editorial that at the end of the war there had 'flowered a widespread active curiosity about our history, and particularly the history of our towns and villages, our own families, schools and businesses. It is time therefore that there was a periodical devoted to historical enquiry as a popular activity. Without guidance to the evidence available and how to use it, the untrained researcher is obliged to grope his way slowly, overlooking much that lies in his way and misinterpreting many of the discoveries he makes. The genealogist needs to study the place in which his ancestors lived; the local historian draws much of his information from archaeology and family records; the chronicler of school and business finds many keys to their story in personalities.' So the journal would give 'the reader guidance among records and archaeological material. It will include articles on the social background of our predecessors of varying classes, occupations and places. It will keep in mind the special needs of people working in groups, the local historical and archaeological societies.'[43] *The Local Historian* flourished, celebrating its fiftieth anniversary in 2002, largely because successive editors followed, through changing circumstances as best they could, the principles laid down by FitzHugh in 1952.

I became editor of *The Amateur Historian* in April 1955 and continued until November 1975, the longest stint of any editor. In November 1975 the Chairman and Secretary of the Publications Sub-Committee of the Standing Conference for Local History, then the publishers of *The Local Historian*, summarised its history to date: 'In 1955, the journal was just over two and a half years old. Since then, Mr Munby has seen the journal through three changes of publisher and five printers. He has been party to overcoming many crises; there was a gap of fifteen months in which no number was published. This hiatus was ended in 1961 when the Standing Conference for Local History was able to persuade its parent body, the National Council of Social Service, to accept responsibility for publishing the magazine. Throughout his period of twenty years unpaid service, Mr Munby has adhered to the policy underlying the journal which is to provide its readers with material on methods of research, sources of historical information and background matter for further study. In this long period, the study of local history has changed fundamentally in character and has thus demanded editorial flexibility. Mr Munby has throughout been closely in touch with keen amateurs cooperating in the writing of local histories as well as with equally ardent professionals asking new questions and finding new methods of response'.[44] During my editorship the two most important events were the taking over of responsibility for publication by the Standing Conference in 1961 and the change of name to *The Local Historian* in 1968.

This was a long considered and carefully prepared operation. In 1965 the journal contained an addressed but unstamped postcard, asking for readers' comments on the editorial approach and contents as well as indicating whether or not they favoured a change of name to *The Local Historian*. There was a remarkable response. Some 20% of readers answered. Replies came from all over Britain and from Australia, Holland, Italy, Mexico and the USA. While 94 preferred to keep the existing title and 17 were indifferent, 212 favoured a change. A full report of the responses was published in 1966 and the change in title announced.

Among the responses were many comments on what has been a perennial source of conflict and confusion among local historians, the false dichotomy between 'amateurs' and 'professionals'. Among local historians this certainly was and, probably, still is a meaningless distinction. There may be professionally trained local historians today but there were none thirty years ago. The professional historians, graduates teaching in secondary schools and universities, were more ignorant of the sources used and problems met by parish historians than was the local 'amateur'. As late at 1971 only nine out of forty-two universities and polytechnics offered local history as an undergraduate option, and in no case was it compulsory. By 1975 twenty universities and nine polytechnics, 37 out of 90 higher educational institutions, reported that they were teaching local history to undergraduates and in eight cases it was compulsory. However local history was not seen as Finberg or Hoskins saw it, important in its own right. It was, primarily, thought of as a means of introducing students to research techniques.

Almost half of the authors of the articles published by the two recent editors of *The Local Historian*, Philip Morgan and Margaret Bonney, between 1988 and 2001, were unconnected with the world of academic history. They included civil servants, a solicitor, a prison governor, a mariner-pilot, and a taxi driver. Of course many such non-professional contributors had had all kinds of training in the study of local history.

In 1984, thanks to the initiative and enterprise of Susan and Robert Howard of Nottingham, another journal, *Local History*, now *Local History Magazine*, began its long and useful life. It is admirably complementary to *The Local Historian*. It usually appears six times a year. Its aims have been 'to promote local history in all its forms among as many people as possible, and to encourage local historians to communicate with each other and with the widest possible public, so that the relevance of local history to all sections of the community can generally be appreciated'. *The Local History Magazine*'s contents cover so many aspects of the local historian's world, 'learning from one another's experiences', as the editors explained in 1986.[45] There is a great deal of information about developments and activities, about publications and publishing, and about people who are or have been active as local historians, almost none of which appears in *The Local Historian*, though some has been printed in BALH's *Local History News*. The Howards' *Local History Magazine* as it now is has almost become the local historians' house magazine while *The Local Historian* is more like their Transactions.

Another point of view: regionalism

So far in this account it is the 'Leicester School approach' which has predominated, but there were other views among active local historians. 'The Leicester School approach is unsuited to much modern local history, Dr Hoskins and his associates have not much sympathy with the rise of modern industry.' 'The parish does become increasingly inappropriate as a boundary of study as one approaches modern times, the nineteenth and twentieth centuries'. These were the views of Donald Read expressed in a controversy on 'The Use of Local History', started by John Marshall in the *The Amateur Historian* in 1963.[46] Marshall put forward an alternative view of local history. The essence of his argument was that 'while Dr Finberg makes an admirable case for the study of the local community ... it is disturbing to see the emphasis put on a geographical boundary, that of the parish. [There were] limiting and harmful effects which could follow the artifical confinement of the local historian within parish boundaries.' 'Let us have far more emphasis on regional studies and on definite if limited themes within the region.'[47] In 1978 Marshall that argued parish-type history just doesn't wash as a worthwhile exercise. 'It is a fallacy that the material for the history of a village always does a lot to increase one's insights ... It is a good idea to look at one's regional background, no matter what the topic one is studying ... The regional historian has to ... use a dozen specialisms ... in the activity of looking at districts as a whole. He has more chance of doing this in the pursuit of broad themes and topics; to use all the historical techniques available to study a tiny patch of England is to lose one's sense of proportion.'[48]

In 1978 Marshall argued that 'it was in the fifties' that local history took the wrong route. 'English Local History has never really overcome the effects of the agrarian, rural and bucolic impulse and emphasis that it received ... with the momentous beginnings of *The Agrarian History of England* and the first popularisations of so-called landscape history [when] serious localised history gained its main momentum. The confinement of much local history to parish boundaries was cramping and anti-educational.' In 1993 the point was made that the history of industrial colonies had been neglected by local historians 'because the local community has meant the rural village, or just as relevantly, the pre-industrial village'. 'At what critical point does a village transform itself into a town? This is a conundrum which local and urban historians rarely debate, yet it is crucial.'[49]

In a perceptive article, *Communities, Societies, Regions and Local History* published in 1996, Marshall turned to the argument that 'communities interpenetrate one another, producing a much broader society'. 'These neighbourhoods may have their own distinctive territories, those of the *pays* or stretches of roughly homogenous countryside ... Regional study would be impossible without geographical distinctions [but] the topographical frameworks of communities and societies [are only] the beginnings of wisdom ... Local history can be too closely tied to geographical determinism.' It is what people thought about where they lived that matters. 'Local historians throughout Britain must attempt to find out how contemporaries formed their allegiances to particular districts'.[50]

Teamwork was a theme Marshall regularly promoted. In 1978 'the way forward lies in teamwork'. In his last article, from 2001, he described 'a cooperative local history project ... a team working together successfully can be a powerful force in the writing of local history'. A group of local people working together had produced a seventeenth century history of their north Lancashire parish which 'aspired to the best professional standards but was readable to the man or woman in the roadway'. It showed that 'so-called amateurs can train themselves in the various skills that are needed' when working together. Marshall could not resist even in this article introducing references to Prof Ted Royle's emphasis 'that local history is best understood through the context of the region'.[51]

In writing these and other articles in which he showed what the amateur local historian might do and how to do it, Dr John Marshall was drawing on his experience as a student and tutor in the adult education movement for well over half a century. He became Reader in the regional history of N W England in the University of Lancaster and Director of its Centre for N W Regional Studies. He played a major part in founding the Conference of Regional and Local Historians (CORAL) of which he was in turn secretary and chairman.

Urban history
Modern urban local history grew out of the Leicester School. Alan Everitt, who succeeded Hoskins as Professor in charge of the Department in 1968, was the initiator. He had been appointed to a research fellowship in urban history in 1960 and published *Change in the Provinces: the Seventeenth Century*, in 1969. In this he commented on 'the remarkable expansion of market towns between 1570 and 1640, and especially the rise of county capitals. Towns were the places where the inhabitants of the region met - to buy, to sell, and to talk.' In 1973 he published *Perspectives in English Urban History*.[52] A useful, comprehensive survey of later publications is the Historical Association's 'Appreciations in History' pamphlet No. 7 by Angus McInnes of 1980, *The English Town 1660-1760*. In 1974 a volume of 'Essays in English Regional History in Honour of W G Hoskins' contained a second part on Urban Growth. This included an essay on 'the building of Bath, 1700-1793' and another on 'the East End of Leeds, 1771-1803'. This Leicester work on urban history was only concerned with development before the industrial revolution.[53]

It is no coincidence that one of the earliest studies of a modern, post-industrial revolution town is John Marshall's *Furness and the Industrial Revolution*, published in 1958 and, significantly, not by an academic or commercial publisher but by the local Library and Museum committee. This is a substantial and scholarly local history of 460 pages. In his epilogue Dr Marshall commented that 'no balanced history of any locality can be constructed from business records' alone, a wise warning that so many of the later in-house histories have neglected. Marshall went on 'the story so far has been complex enough in all conscience, and has called for the use of municipal, industrial and trade union sources; of railway records, parliamentary reports and committees, and private diaries. But it may be doubted whether the foregoing narrative has taken us very far into the minds and hearts of men. The labourers and artisans of mid-Victorian times remain shadowy figures'.[54]

Their descendents can be better studied because there are living memories and better documentation. Marshall's comments on his own magnum opus explain why he has had no amateur followers. The history of industrialised towns has been too considerable a topic for the non-professional. There have been real local studies, however, of the 'labourers and artisans' to whom Marshall referred, as we shall see.

In 1963 Asa Briggs published his *Victorian Cities*, a study of Manchester, Leeds, Birmingham, Middlesbrough, Melbourne in Australia, and 'London: the world city'. The period covered falls between the coming of the railway and the coming of the automobile. This classic underlined the point that no amateur could attempt such complex studies.[55] The kind of sophisticated problems which face the historian of the modern industrial town were tackled in John Foster's *Class Struggle and the Industrial Revolution*. This 1974 Marxist study of 'early industrial capitalism' in Oldham, Northampton and South Shields is, as Eric Hobsbawm describes it in a Foreword, 'an enquiry into certain central features of British industrial development, and into the nature of both the Victorian bourgeoisie and the working class - it is not a piece of local history.'[56] This comment is a clear indication of what happened to local historical studies in the third quarter of the twentieth century. They became test beds for national historians to study a theory, no longer studies of localities for themselves, in their own right.

The one aspect of post-industrial England which had 'possibilities worth examining' by local historians was suggested by H J Dyos, author of *Victorian Suburb*, in an article in *The Amateur Historian* in 1960: 'the most striking demographic feature of twentieth century Britain is the growth of the suburbs. The natural point of departure for more and more amateur historians interested in local history is not only to shift away from the countryside towards the towns but to move right into the suburbs.'[57] In the article quoted Dyos gave splendid advice on how to set about such a study and followed this with considerable information on sources. Though Dyos hoped local historians would follow his example, few did so.

The topics which local historians could and did study were the histories of the 'labourers and artisans', of whom Marshall wrote, in particular Chartism. There have been many local studies: of East Anglia in 1951, of Bradford in 1969, and Essex and Suffolk in 1982, for example. *Our History* published *Chartism in the Black Country* in 1965-66 and several other issues about local working class history, for example *Sheffield Shop Stewards 1916-18* and the *General Strike in the North East*. There was an intense argument about working class history published in a *History Workshop Series* volume in 1981.[58]

This is in no way a full account of local history in England. It is chronologically unbalanced, concentrating on the third quarter of the twentieth century because, from personal experience, I know these years best. Also because this was when local history came of age thanks, particularly, to the work of the Department of Local History at Leicester University. As has been shown it changed from being the pursuit of gentry and clergy to become of popular interest among more ordinary people, breaking into the previously closed precincts of academe. From all sorts of backgrounds large numbers of local historians are now academically trained and have become researchers, lecturers and leaders of local societies, strengthening our understanding of the past - and surely they will continue to do so.

Notes

1 *The Court Hand Restored*, 1949 impression, p. V.
2 Osbert Lancaster, *Draynflete Revealed*, 1951 reprint, p. 16.
3 Peter Laslett, *The Poverty of History*, Cambridge, Opinion, 1961, pp. 15, 17 & 13.
4 W C Sellar and R J Yeatman, *1066 and all that*, Methuen 1930, Penguin 1960 edition pp. 5 & 33-34.
5 *The Historical Association 1906-1956*, Historical Association, 1955, pp. 30, 31, 32. The bibliography was updated and appeared in 1947 as *Local History Handlist: a select bibliography*; it contains many pre-1939 publications.
6 *Local History as a Village Interest* 1938 p. 1.
7 From a manuscript in the possession of Lionel Munby whose uncle, R V Lennard, was a pioneer WEA tutor and attended this conference.
8 Rev A Clark of the Rectory, Great Leighs, Essex to Mr Harry Taylor; Clark's papers are in Lincoln College, Oxford and in the Bodleian. J Munson (ed), *Echoes of the Great War: the Diary of the Rev. Andrew Clark 1914-19*, Oxford, 1985.
9 S G Thicknesse, *Abbots Langley*, Staples, 1946. p. 7.
10 W G Hoskins, *Midland England*, pp. 61 & 67.
11 W E Tate *The Parish Chest*, CUP 1946, 1951, p. VIII.
12 In comments made on a report which I made in 1965 on 'The Teaching of Local History'. BEMS AM/7/65/217.
13 Hertfordshire Archives & Local Studies, AHH 21/4.
14 David Cox in *The Amateur Historian*, Vol 6 No 8 pp. 260-261.
15 From the blurb advertising the forthcoming volume, which contains (p. 3) an outline of Tate's unusual academic career. M E Turner was the editor and compiler of this mammoth work.

16 From a Telediphone Recording, No. 3 in a series: 'Introduction to Archives', made on 17 March 1964, in the possession of Lionel Munby.

17 'Chilterns to Black Country' and 'East Midlands'. Nos 5 & 8 in *About Britain*, Collins 1951; *Devonshire Studies* by W G Hoskins and H P R Finberg, Cape 1952; *Devon*, Collins 1954; *The Making of the English Landscape*, Hodder and Stoughton 1955; *Leicestershire*, Hodder and Stoughton 1957; *The Midland Peasant*, Macmillan 1957; *Devon and its People*, David and Charles 1959; *Local History in England*, Longmans 1959, 1972; *Provincial England*, Macmillan 1963; with Dudley Stamp, *The Common Lands of England and Wales*, Collins 1963; *Fieldwork in Local History*, Faber & Faber 1967, 1969. For Hoskins' many other publications see *English Local History at Leicester 1948 & 1978*: a bibliography, University of Leicester 1981.

18 *Local History in England*, p. XI, the Preface, and from an anonymously published review, presumably in the *Times Literary Supplement*, 'History in Field and Village'. The offprint which I have is endorsed by my uncle, R V Lennard, the author of the review: 'the title was [changed by] the editor. I'd chosen "The Study of Local History"'.

19 *Tavistock Abbey*, CUP 1951; *Devonshire Studies*, Cape 1952; *The Local Historian and his Theme*, Leicester Occasional Papers 1952; Editor, *Agricultural History Review* 1953-64; *Early Charters of Devon and Cornwall*, Occasional Papers 1953; *Roman and Saxon Withington*: a Study in Continuity, Leicester Occasional Papers No 8 1955; *Gloucestershire: the History of the Landscape*, Hodder and Stoughton 1955, 1975; General editor, *The Agrarian History of England and Wales*, 1956-74; *Gloucestershire Studies*, Leicester UP 1957; *Early Charters of the West Midlands*, Leicester UP 1961; *Local History in the University*: inaugural lecture, Leicester UP 1964; *Lucerna: some problems in the early history of England*, Macmillan 1964; *Early Charters of Wessex*, Leicester UP 1964; Finberg & V H T Skipp, *Local History: objective and pursuit*, David and Charles 1967; *West Country Historical Studies*, David and Charles 1969; Editor, *The Agrarian History of England and Wales* Vol. 1. AD 43-1042, CUP 1972; *Formation of England 550-1042*, Hart-Davis, MacGibbon 1976.

20 From Tape Number TLO 83313, an edited version of a Transcript Telediphone recording made between 2.15 and 4.0 pm on Friday 11 May 1962, in the possession of Lionel Munby.

21 *Local History: objective and pursuit*, pp. 32, 33 & 59.

22 Joan Thirsk 'Nature versus Nurture' in *History Workshop Journal*, 47, Spring 1999, p. 275.

23 *Ibid.*, p. 277.

24 *Fenland Farming in the Sixteenth Century*, Leicester Occasional Papers, 1953; *English Peasant Farming: the Agrarian History of Lincolnshire from Tudor to Recent Times*, Routledge, 1957; *Suffolk Farming in the Nineteenth Century*, Suffolk Records Society, 1958; *Tudor Enclosures*, Historical Association, 1959; Editor, *Agricultural History Review*, 1964-72; *Sources of Information on Population 1500-1760*, Phillimore, 1965; Editor and contributor to *The Agrarian History of England and Wales*, Vol. IV,

1500-1640, CUP, 1967; Editor and contributor to *ibid.*, Vol. V Parts I & II. 1640-1750. CUP, 1984; 'Land, Church and People: essays presented to Professor H P R Finberg', *Agricultural History Review Supplement*, 1970; Editor, *Seventeenth Century Economic Documents*, Clarendon Press, 1972; General editor, *The Agrarian History of England and Wales*, 1975; *The Restoration*, Longmans, 1976; *Economic Policy and Projects: the development of a consumer society in early modern England*, Clarendon Press, 1978. Joan Thirsk published very many articles on a wide range of subjects and from 1953 annual lists of publications on agrarian history. *Alternative Agriculture: from the Black Death to the present day*, 1999.

25 *History Workshop Journal*, 47, p. 275.
26 Joan Thirsk, *Fenland Farming in the 16th Century*, p. 3.
27 Quoted from *History* on cover of *Alternative Agriculture*.
28 *History Workshop Journal*, 47, pp. 274, 273.
29 K J Allison, M W Beresford, J G Hurst *The Deserted Villages of Oxfordshire*, Leicester Occasional Papers, 1965; *Northamptonshire*, 1966; *The Lost Villages of England*, 1954; *History on the Ground*, Lutterworth, 1957; with J K S St Joseph, *Medieval England: an aerial survey*, CUP, 1958; *New Towns of the Middle Ages: town plantation in England, Wales and Gascony*, Lutterworth, 1967; with John G Hurst *Deserted Medieval Villages*, Lutterworth, 1971.
30 M W Beresford, *History on the Ground*, p. 13.
31 From a Telediphone Recording made on 5 March 1964 for a series 'Introduction to Archives', No. 4: 'Town History and Town Archives', of which the author was chairman. In the possession of Lionel Munby.
32 Margaret Spufford. *Contrasting Communities: English villagers in the sixteenth and seventeenth centuries*, CUP, 1974, pp. 165, 166, 351, 352.
33 Robert Douch, *Handbook of Local History*, Dorset, 1952; R B Pugh, *How to Write a Parish History* (an update of J C Cox's book of 1909, long out of print), 1954; Francis Celoria, *Teach Yourself Local History*, 1958; Joscelyne Finberg, *Exploring Villages*, 1959; Eileen A Gooder, *Latin for Local History*, 1961; M. W. Barley *The English Farmhouse and Cottage*, 1961; L M Munby, editor, 'Short Guides to Records', appeared in *History* from 1961; W R Powell, *Local History from Blue Books*, 1962; John West, *Village Records*, 1962.

By the 1970s so many books and booklets were being published that it became difficult to choose between them: Alan Rogers, *This was their World: approaches to History* (to accompany BBC programmes), 1972; W B Stephens, *Sources for English Local History*, 1973; David Iredale, *Discovering Local History*, 1973; David Iredale, *Enjoying Archives*, 1973; *Local History Research and Writing*, 1974; David Dymond, *Archaeology and History*, 1974; *Writing a Church Guide*, 1977; *Writing Local History*, 1981; John Richardson, *The Local Historian's Encyclopaedia*, 1974; Alan Rogers, *Group Projects in Local History*, 1977; J S Moore, *Avon Local History Handbook*, 1979.

34 Deserted Medieval Village Research Group (DMVRG) 1952; Vernacular Architectural Group 1952; British Agricultural History Society 1953*; Railway and Canal Historical Society 1954; Society for Medieval Archaeology 1957*; Victorian Society 1958; Society for the Study of Labour History 1960; Society for Folk Life Studies 1961; Historic Metallurgy Group 1962; Urban History Society 1962-63*; Furniture History Society 1964; Veterinary History Society 1964; Cambridge Group for the History of Population and Social Structure 1964; British Costume Society 1965; Garden History Society 1965*; History of Education Society 1967*; Vernacular Architecture Society 1970*; Oral History Society 1972; Moated Sites Research Group 1973; Local Population Studies Society 1973*; Federation of Family History Societies 1974; Society for the Interpretation of Britain's Heritage 1975; Social History Society 1976; International Society for the Study of Church Monuments 1978; Society for Landscape Studies 1979. (Those societies marked * produced their own journals or bulletins)
35 *English local history at Leicester* 1948-78, compiled by Alan Everitt and Margery Tranter 1981 p.XXVII
36 Ed. Bernard Jennings, *A History of Nidderdale*, written by the Pateley Bridge Local History Tutorial class, Advertiser Press, Huddersfield 1967; ed. Bernard Jennings, *A History of Harrogate and Knaresborough*, written by the Harrogate WEA Local History Group, Advertiser Press, Huddersfield 1970; R Fieldhouse & B Jennings, *A History of Richmond & Swaledale*, Phillimore 1978.
37 E P Thompson, *The Making of the English Working Class*, Pelican, 1968, p. 14.
38 Edward Gillett and Kenneth A MacMahon, *A History of Hull*, OUP, 1980.
39 Barrie Trinder, *The Industrial Revolution in Shropshire*, Phillimore, 1973. *The Making of the Industrial Landscape*, 1982, Phoenix, 1997.
40 *English Local History Handlist: a short bibliography and list of sources* (H.69). 1947, 1952, 1965, 1969, by F W Kuhlicke and F G Emmison; F G Emmison and I Gray (revised edition), *County Records* (H.62) 1961; W R Powell *Local History from Blue Books* (H.64) 1962; A A Dibben, *Title Deeds*, (H.72) 1968; Peter Eden, *Smaller Houses in England 1520-1820*, (H.75) 1969; Joyce Youings, *Local Record Sources in Print and in Progress*, 1972-76, (H.85) 1972, 1973, 1977; F G Emmison, *How to Read Local Archives 1550-1700*, (H.82) 1973; Lionel M Munby (general editor), *Short Guides to Records 1-24*, Historical Association 1972, with additional bibliography and new Preface by Dr K M Thompson, 1994; Dr K M Thompson (general editor), *Short Guides to Records*, second series 25-48, Historical Association, 1997.
41 Eric Hobsbawm 'The Historians' Group of the Communist Party' in ed. Maurice Cornforth *Rebels and their Causes*, 1978.
42 *The Luddites and Other Essays*, Michael Katanka, 1971.
43 *The Amateur Historian*, Vol. 1, No. 1, p. 1. See also *The Local Historian*, Vol. 22, No. 1, pp. 6-7.
44 *The Local Historian*, Vol. 11, No. 8, p. 439.

45 *Local History*, No. 13, Nov/Dec 1986, p. 3, and letter dated 20 Dec 2002 to Lionel Munby from The Local History Press Ltd.
46 *The Amateur Historian*, Vol. 6, No. 4, pp. 123, 121.
47 *Ibid.*, No. 1, p. 12; No. 7, p. 234; No. 1. p. 17.
48 *The Local Historian*, Vol. 13, No. 1, pp. 7, 8, 9 & 10.
49 *Ibid.*, Vol. 22, No. 1, pp. 14 & 17; Vol. 23, No. 3, pp. 146 & 152.
50 *Ibid.*, Vol. 26, No. 1, pp. 37, 38 & 39.
51 *Ibid.*, Vol. 13, No. 1, p. 9; Vol. 31, No. 2, pp. 66, 80, 82 & 79.
52 Alan Everitt, *Change in the Provinces: the 17th Century*, Leics. UP, 1969, p. 24; Alan Everitt, *Perspectives in English Urban History*, MacMillan, 1973, and many articles in *The Local Historian*, Vols VIII and XI.
53 Ed. C W Chalklin & M. A. Havinden, *Rural Change and Urban Growth 1500-1800*, Longman, 1974.
54 John Marshall *Furness and the industrial revolution: an economic history of Furness (1711-1900) and the town of Barrow (1757-1897)*, Barrow-in-Furness Library and Museum Committee, 1958, p. 425.
55 Asa Briggs, *Victorian Cities*, Odhams Press, 1963, p. 13.
56 John Foster, *Class Struggle and the Industrial Revolution: early industrial capitalism in three English towns*, Weidenfeld & Nicolson, 1974, Methuen, 1977, 1979. Foreword 2nd page, no numbers.
57 H J Dyos, 'The Annals of Suburbia' in *The Amateur Historian*, Vol. 4, No. 7, Spring 1960, p. 275. F M L Thompson's *Hampstead: building a borough 1650-1965*, Routledge, 1974, traces the development of a middle class suburb.
58 *Chartism in East Anglia*, WEA Eastern District, duplicated 1951; A J Peacock, *Bradford Chartism 1838-1840*, St Anthony's Press, York, 1969; A F J Brown, *Chartism in Essex and Suffolk*, Essex Record Office & Suffolk Libraries and Archives, 1982; George Barnsby, 'Chartism in the Black Country 1850-1860', *Our History*, 40, Winter 1965-66; Bill Moore, 'Sheffield Shop Stewards in the First World War 1916-18', *Our History*, 18, Summer, 1960; Various, 'The General Strike in the North-East'. *Our History*, 22, Summer 1961; Ed. Raphael Samuel, *People's History and Socialist Theory*, Routledge, 1981, pp. 21-48.

Local History Studies in Wales

D Huw Owen

Introduction
Many activities and publications directed towards furthering local history studies in the British Isles are of relevance for those working on a specific locality within Wales, and this is not unexpected in view of the political and administrative history of Wales. Repositories and organisations operating beyond the boundaries of Wales have for various reasons collected material or information relating to Wales, and of particular value for the local historian in Wales are the collections of the British Library and the National Archives, and the *International Genealogical Index* compiled by members of the Mormon Church.

General reference works in this subject area assist local historians in Wales, and include those volumes which refer specifically to England, for example W G Hoskins, *Local History in England* (2nd ed. reprinted 1976) and W B Stephens, *Sources for English Local History* (2nd ed. 1981). Welsh local historians have contributed to societies and co-operative publishing ventures whose scope extends beyond Wales, and benefited from the contents of the journals and volumes thereby produced. At the same time, social and cultural characteristics developed over an extended period of time, together with a heightened sense of national identity have contributed to a distinctive tradition of local history studies within Wales.

One important aspect is associated with the well-established literary and historiographical tradition expressed through the medium of the Welsh language. A feature of Welsh-language poetry composed from the Dark Ages to the present day is that of praising a specific locality. In the Later Middle Ages itinerant bards eulogised their patrons and their homes, and hospitality was provided for itinerant poets at Cottrell, the home of Rice Merrick (c. 1520-1586/7). His *Morganiae Archaiographia, A Book of the Antiquities of Glamorganshire*, compiled during the period 1574-1584, was edited by Brian Ll James and published by the South Wales Record Society in 1983.

Historical texts
In recent years other older historical texts have been re-published, including in 1978 the latest translation, with introduction, by Lewis Thorpe, of Gerald of Wales's two works *The Journey of Wales*, and *The Description of Wales*, comprising detailed descriptions of a number of places visited during his tour of Wales in 1188. George Owen's *The Description of Pembrokeshire* (1603), ed. Dillwyn Miles, was published by Gomer Press in 1994. Owen's map of Pembrokeshire, drawn in 1602, was published by his friend William Camden in the 1610 edition of *Britannia*.

The latter volume also seems to have influenced Sir John Wynn of Gwydir, near Llanrwst (1553-1627). A scholar and bardic patron, his volume on the history of his family (1770) was published by Gomer Press as *The History of the Gwydir Family and Memoirs*, ed. J Gwynfor Jones (1990). Camden's influence on Welsh antiquarians continued into the second half of the eighteenth century, with the edition of *Britannia* (1789) containing contributions by Thomas Pennant of Downing, Flintshire (1726-1798). His *History of the parishes of Whiteford and Holywell* (1796) was reprinted in 1988 by the Clwyd County Council, Library and Museum Service, and an abridged version of his *Tours in Wales* (1784) was published by Gwasg Carreg Gwalch in 1998. Pennant had concentrated on north Wales, but contemporary information on south Wales was provided by Benjamin Heath Malkin (1769-1842), whose *The Scenery, Antiquities and Biography of South Wales* (1804), was reprinted by S. R. Publishers Ltd. in 1970.

Historical societies

Recent publications and an ambitious research project have emphasised the significant contribution to Welsh historical studies of two London-based literary and patriotic societies, established in the eighteenth century. Glenda Carr's study in 1983 of William Owen Pughe (1759-1835) drew attention to the work of this prominent member of the Gwyneddigion – the London society for people from North Wales. Another leading member was Edward Williams, known as Iolo Morganwg (1747-1826), the poet and antiquary whose over-enthusiastic promotion of the importance of both the bardic tradition and the traditions of his native county of Glamorgan resulted in the fabrication of historical sources. A team of researchers based at the University of Wales Centre for Advanced Welsh and Celtic Studies, Aberystwyth, is currently preparing a series of publications focused on Iolo's diverse interests and activities. The other society associated with the London-Welsh community was the Honourable Society of Cymmrodorion, established in 1751, and revived in 1820 and 1873, and which continues to be active today. The society has promoted and published scholarly works including significant studies in local history. It published the journal *Y Cymmrodor* from 1877 to 1951, the *Dictionary of Welsh Biography* (1959 and 2001) and the *Transactions* of the society from 1893 to the present day.

Within Wales the earliest scholarly society which continues to flourish is the Cambrian Archaeological Association, established in 1846 for the study and the preservation of the antiquities of Wales. The journal *Archaeologia Cambrensis* contains material on genealogy, heraldry, toponomy, folklore and literature, reports on the society's excavations, and a review of periodical literature in the preceding year. A county history society operates in each one of the historic counties of Wales, that is the thirteen shires which functioned from 1536 to 1974. Journals are published regularly, normally on an annual basis, and include scholarly articles examining various aspects of the history of the county and often accompanied by illustrative material. The oldest of these societies is The Powysland Club, whose journal *The Montgomeryshire Collections* has been published since 1868, and which has published in recent years a number of volumes including *The Historical Atlas of Montgomeryshire* (1991). Journals produced by other well-established local societies include the *Transactions of the Neath Antiquarian Society* and *Gower*, and the Cynon Valley History Society published the volume *Cynon Coal* in 2001.

Book reviews appear in most of the journals, and information is also provided on those publications for which the society has been responsible, for example A D Carr, *Medieval Anglesey* (1982) [Anglesey Antiquarian Society and Field Club], and Eiluned Rees (ed.), *Carmarthenshire Memories of the Twentieth Century* (2002) [Carmarthenshire Antiquarian Society]. Other regular features include information on local museums and record offices and reports on the activities of the four archaeological trusts which cover the counties of Clwyd-Powys, Glamorgan-Gwent, Gwynedd and Dyfed. Publications which result directly from the work of these trusts include E G T James, *Carmarthen, An archaeological and topographical survey* (1980), and D M Robinson, *South Glamorgan's Heritage* (1985). Information is also provided in the journals on the membership and activities of the society, with reports of lectures, meetings and field excursions arranged during the year, and specific projects such as the Carmarthenshire Place-Name Survey.

Indexes to the journals are published periodically by several societies. Recent issues of *Brycheiniog*, the journal of the Brecknock Society and Museum Friends, have contained a detailed index. A cumulative index to volumes 1-31 of the *Transactions of the Denbighshire Historical Society* appeared in volume 32 (1983), and a title index to volumes 32-47 in volume 48 (1999). A comprehensive index, compiled by Andrew Green, listing authors, persons, places, objects and topics mentioned in the *Transactions of the Carmarthenshire Antiquarian Society*, from 1905 to 1977, was published by the society as a separate publication in 1981, with a further supplement covering the period 1978-1987. In 1988 the Flintshire Historical Society published separately a detailed index to volumes 1-11 of the *Journal* (1911-25) and volumes 1-2 of the *Record Series*, prepared by Dennis Roberts.

Some county history societies have occasionally published record sources. In 1982 the South Wales Record Society was established to publish editions of records relating to the history of South Wales. Reference has already been made to the publication in 1983 of Rice Merrick's *Morganiae Archaiographia*, and other publications include *The Diary of William Thomas, of Michaelston-Super-Ely, near St. Fagans, Glamorgan, 1762-1795*, ed. R T W Denning (1995) and *Letter Book of John Byrd,: Custom Collector in South-East Wales, 1648-80*, ed. Stephen K Roberts (1999).

Family history
Several historical societies in Wales are directed towards specific interest groups, but the journals produced promote an awareness of records which are often of

general relevance for local historians. Six family history societies are active in Wales, in Clwyd, Gwynedd, Powys, Dyfed, Glamorgan and Gwent. Regular meetings are held, and projects sponsored include the transcription of monumental inscriptions in churches and graveyards, the transcription and indexing of parish registers, and the preparation of census indexes. The Clwyd Family History Society's Centre, opened at Ruthin in 1988, provides access to a range of family and local history sources. The Association of Family History Societies of Wales co-operates closely with the Federation of Family History Societies, and the two bodies jointly published *Welsh Family History: A Guide to Research*, ed. John Rowlands, *et al* (1993). In 1999 the Federation published, in conjunction with the Department of Continuing Education, University of Wales Aberyswyth, *Secona Stages in Researching Welsh Ancestry*, eds John & Sheila Rowlands. The numerous publications of the Federation, including the official journal, *Family History News and Digest*, provide valuable information and assistance for Welsh family historians.

Religious history
The historical societies of the various religious denominations, including the Welsh Baptists and Independents, The Presbyterian Church of Wales and the Methodist Church in Wales continue to publish journals with many, but not all of the articles in these journals in the Welsh language. *The Journal of the Historical Society of the Church in Wales*, and the *Journal of Welsh Ecclesiastical History* have been superseded by the *Journal of Welsh Religious History*, published since 1993, and with a new series launched in 2001. CAPEL, the Chapels Heritage Society, established in 1986 to encourage the study and preservation of the Nonconformist heritage of Wales, has published twice a year a *Newsletter* and an information leaflet featuring chapel buildings in a selected locality visited by the society: recent issues feature chapels in Abergele, Llangefni, Bala, Brecon, Blaenavon, and Caerphilly.

Labour history
The Society for the Study of Welsh Labour History, founded in 1970, has fostered research into, and the teaching of the history of the working class in Wales. The journal *Llafur* has been published since 1972 and contains scholarly articles and also reports on meetings and activities organised by, and involving the society. The chronological range of recent articles extends from a study of the mariners' strike of 1336 in north Wales (1997), to the attempt to form a workers' co-operative at Cwmllynfell Colliery (1997). Reports from the South Wales Miners' Library frequently appeared in *Llafur*. Printed material, the oral history and video collections, posters and banners housed at the Library form part of the South Wales Coalfield Collection, which, recording the social, economic and cultural experience of the South Wales coalfield, is held at the University of Wales,

Swansea with manuscripts and photographs housed at the Library and Information Centre.

Adult education

Local historians in Wales have undoubtedly benefited from courses organised by the University of Wales and the Open University. The University of Wales has over an extended period encouraged adult education and classes specialising in local history have been held by Departments of Extra-Mural Studies, or, as they have been designated in recent years, Departments of Continuing Education. A part-time, two-year Diploma course in Local History has been organised by the University of Wales Cardiff since 1979, and a part-time, three-year MA course in Local History since 1994. Details of the subjects of Diploma in Local History dissertations relating to Glamorgan, together with those produced for the part-time, two-year Diploma in Local History course offered at the University of Wales Swansea were printed in *Morgannwg*, XXXV (1991). The University institutions at Aberystwyth and Bangor organise adult education classes in west, mid and north Wales, and many of these courses offer certificates within an accreditation system. Material gleaned from classes held in south Ceredigion by the Department of Extra Mural Studies, Aberystwyth was used by the tutor, David Jenkins, as the basis for his volume, *The Agricultural Community in South West Wales at the turn of the Twentieth Century* (1971).

In North Wales the Department in the University at Bangor responsible for adult education has co-operated closely with the Workers Educational Association, which has over the years encouraged local history as part of its responsibilities for adult education. The WEA has also been extremely active in South Wales, and one of the most active branches, at Llanelli, has organised classes on a wide range of subjects, including local history, since 1914. The branch has also published annually since 1986 *Amrywiaeth Llanelli Miscellany*, and also the volume *Footprints of Faith*, a series of lectures on the Anglican Church and Nonconformity in Llanelli delivered to classes organised by the branch in 1987-88. Four lectures delivered under the auspices of the Association in Merthyr Tydfil were published by the University of Wales Press in the volume *Merthyr Politics: the Making of a Working-class Tradition*, ed. Glanmor Williams (1966).

The University of Wales

The University of Wales Press, founded in 1922, has made an immense contribution to scholarship in Wales, and facilitated the study of local history by means of its many monographs, texts and journals. Recent volumes include David W Howell, *The Rural Poor in Eighteenth-Century Wales* (2000) and Gareth Williams, *Valleys of Song, Music and Society in Wales, 1840-1914* (reprinted 2003); and the five English-language, five Welsh-language and one bilingual volumes in the 'Social History of the Welsh Language' series, ed. Geraint H Jenkins (1998-2001) contain detailed studies of the social context of the history of the Welsh language in various communities. Monographs in the *Studies in Welsh History* series include Keith Gildart, *North Wales Miners, A Fragile Unity, 1945-1996* (2001) and Mari Williams, *A Forgotten Army, Female Munitions Workers of South Wales, 1939-1945* (2002).

The University's Board of Celtic Studies has been responsible for a number of important series of publications, and its History and Law Committee has published major groups of historical records including *The Religious Census of 1851, Vol.1, South Wales* eds Ieuan Gwynedd Jones and David Williams (1976); and *Vol. 2 North Wales*, ed. Ieuan Gwynedd Jones (1981). The journal *Welsh History Review*, published twice a year since 1960, often contains articles concentrating on specific localities, such as those relating to Llanelli, Newport and Swansea in Vol. 21, No. 3 (June 2003). A list of periodical articles published in a wide range of periodicals also appears every year. *The Bulletin of the Board of Celtic Studies* was published from 1921 until 1993, with an index, compiled by Simon Rodway, in 2003. In 1993 the *Bulletin* was amalgamated with *Studia Celtica* which had appeared since 1966. The University's Social Studies Committee published *The National Atlas of Wales*, ed. H Carter, in 1988.

County histories

The University Press has been involved in the publication of the history of individual counties. In 1988 *Cardiganshire County History Volume 3: Cardiganshire in Modern Times*, eds Geraint H Jenkins and Ieuan Gwynedd Jones was published, and in 2001 a reprint of Volume 1, *From the Earliest Times to the Coming of the Normans*, eds. J L Davies and D P Kirby. The first volume, *Gwent in Prehistory and Early History*, eds Miranda Aldhouse-Green and Ray Howell, of the proposed five-volume *Gwent County History*, ed. Ralph A Griffiths, was published by the press in 2004. The tradition whereby local authorities assisted efforts to publish official county histories was illustrated by the publication of the six-volume history of Glamorgan: this venture, initiated in 1930, was completed in 1988 with the publication of *Glamorgan County History, Vol. VI, Glamorgan Society 1780-1980*, ed. Prys Morgan. Two volumes of the *History of Merioneth* have been published, Vol. I: *From the Earliest Times to the Age of the Native Princes*, eds. E G Bowen and C A Gresham in 1967, and Vol. II, *The Middle Ages*, eds J Beverley Smith and Llinos Beverley Smith in 2001; and three volumes of the *History of Pembrokeshire*: Vol. 3, *Early Modern Pembrokeshire 1536-1815*, ed. B E Howells (1987), Vol. 4, *Modern Pembrokeshire, 1815-1974*, ed. D W Howell (1993), and *Medieval Pembrokeshire*, ed. R F Walker, (2002). In 2002 the Carmarthenshire County Council published R S Craig, R Protheroe Jones, and M V Symons, *The Industrial and Maritime History of Llanelly and Burry Port 1750-2000*. Volumes chronicling the history of cities and towns include *Barry, The Centenary Book*, ed. D Moore (2nd ed.

1985); *Swansea, An Illustrated History*, ed. Glanmor Williams (1990), and W S K Thomas, *Brecon, 1093-1660: An Illustrated History* (1991).

Archive services

Local authorities also support the archive, library and museum services for which they are responsible. A significant trend in recent years has been the co-ordination of activities whose separate identity had previously been carefully safeguarded, and the A N Palmer Centre for Local Studies and Archives in Wrexham County Borough Museum now houses the main Local Studies Collection transferred from Wrexham Library, together with the existing Archives Service. Archive services are provided for all the Welsh counties, and the collections most frequently consulted by local historians in local record offices include Quarter Session records. Their value was emphasised in *Denbighshire Quarter Session Records*, ed. A G Veysey (1991) and which, covering all aspects of local administration before the foundation of county councils in 1889, include land tax assessments, enclosure awards, poll books and electoral registers (after 1832).

Other sources used by the local historian include rate books, parish and Nonconformist records, family and estate papers, also a wide range of educational, industrial and business records, and, especially in the Gwynedd Archives Service, maritime records. Published guides include A G Veysey, *Guide to the Flintshire Record Office* (1974) and Kim Collins, *The West Glamorgan Archive Service. A Guide to the Collections* (1998). Other publications include *A Catalogue of Glamorgan Estate Maps*, compiled by Hilary M. Thomas (1992), published by the Glamorgan Archives Service. The series *Studies in Swansea's History* was launched in 1992 with the publication of two volumes sponsored by the Swansea City Council, one by R T Price on aspects of the history of the Irish community and the other by N A Robins on early twentieth-century housing. Volumes published by the Gwynedd Archives and Museums Service include Eric Jones and David Gwyn, *Dolgarrog, An Industrial History* (1989), and the journal *Cymru a'r Mor/Maritime History*, published since 1976, with No. 24 appearing in 2003.

Libraries

Archive material, together with maps, newspapers, photographs and audio-visual material is also held in public and academic libraries, with extensive collections found at the oldest public libraries, such as those at Cardiff and Swansea. Publishing ventures have been associated with several public libraries. The Llanelli Borough Council published a series of monographs, including M V Symons, *Coal Mining in the Llanelli area, Vol. 1, 16th century to 1829* (1979), prepared by members of the Llanelli Local History Group, based at the town's public library. Important collections are also held by university libraries. Reference has already been made to the South Wales Coalfield Collection, and valuable material relating to estates, mines and quarries in north Wales is housed at the University of Wales, Bangor.

Museums

This university is also responsible for the Museum of Welsh Antiquities and Art Gallery, which incorporates a local history collection in the 'Bangor Room'. The collections and facilities of 131 museums and galleries in Wales are described by J Geraint Jenkins in *Exploring Museums, Wales* (1990), a Museums Association guide. Museums which contain material relating to the history of their locality include the Brecknock Museum, housed in the Shire Hall in the centre of Brecon; the Carmarthen Museum occupying a building used as a palace by the Bishops of St. David's from 1542 until 1974; the Ceredigion Museum in a building previously serving as a theatre and later as a cinema; and the Newport Museum and Art Gallery which shares with the public library a modern purpose-built building in the centre of the town. Specialised museums concerned with specific themes include the Gwent Rural Life Museum, Usk; the Lloyd George Museum, Llanystumdwy; and the Seiont 11 Maritime Museum, Caernarfon.

National Museum and National Library

The National Museums and Galleries of Wales, and the National Library of Wales, both of which were founded in 1907, are two major national institutions which have made a significant contribution in this field on the basis of the scope and value of their collections and publications. The permanent exhibitions housed in the National Museum of Wales, at Cathays Park, Cardiff include 'The Natural History of Wales', tracing the development of the landscape, with attention focused on the marine and woodland environment. Other integral parts of The National Museums and Galleries of Wales include the Museum of Welsh Life, at St. Fagans, near Cardiff, where buildings representing typical features of Welsh life have been re-erected; the Museum of the Welsh Woollen Industry at Dre-fach Felindre, in west Wales; the Big Pit Mining Museum at Blaenavon; and the Welsh Slate Museum at Llanberis. The Museum has published a number of volumes which are valuable for local historians, and these include Jeremy B Lowe, *Welsh country workers' housing, 1775-1875* (reprint, 1985), Gerallt D. Nash, *Workmen's halls and institutions: Oakdale Workmen's Institute* (1995) and Beth Thomas, *Cytiau chwain a phalasau breuddwydion/Fleapits and picture palaces* (1997).

The National Library of Wales, located at Aberystwyth, collects an extensive range of manuscript, printed, cartographic, visual, sound and moving image material relating to Wales and the Celtic peoples. One of the six legal deposit libraries in the United Kingdom and Ireland, the Library has the right to claim almost all British and Irish publications, and recent legislation has extended this right to non-print and electronic publications. This provision is of immense value for local historians in relation to the availability of printed books, periodicals, newspapers, and printed maps. Other sources held by the Library and extensively used by local historians include probate and parish records, estate maps and records, tithe apportionment maps and schedules, antiquarian and 'historic' Ordnance Survey maps, paintings, drawings, prints, photographs, postcards, sound and video recordings, films and recorded radio and television programmes. Information on some of the Library's collections is provided in *Guide to the Department of Manuscripts and Records, The National Library of Wales* (1994) and *Guide to the Department of Pictures and Maps* (1997). *The Journal of the National Library of Wales*, published since 1939, contains scholarly articles and notes on the collections. Other relevant volumes published by the Library include *Cofrestri Plwyf Cymru/Parish Registers of Wales*, eds C J Williams and J Watts-Williams (2nd ed. 2000), *Cofrestri Anghydffurfiol Cymru/Nonconformist Registers*, ed. Dafydd Ifans (1994), and *A Guide to the Records of the Great Sessions in Wales*, ed. Glyn Parry (1995).

Buildings

Two institutions which concentrate largely on the built heritage of Wales are the Royal Commission on Ancient Monuments for Wales, and Cadw: Welsh Historic Monuments. The Royal Commission, established in 1908 to produce an inventory of the ancient and historic monuments of Wales and Monmouthshire, has published at regular intervals inventories of several of the historic counties, including a number of volumes on Glamorgan (1976-2001), and also a book by Stephen Hughes, *Copperopolis. Landscapes of the Early Industrial Period in Swansea* (2000). Handsome and elegant volumes present detailed surveys and descriptions of internal and external features, accompanied by colour and monochrome plates, line-drawings, plans and sections, of an extensive range of buildings and settlements, including hill forts, castles, monastic granges, deserted villages, gentry houses, farmhouses and cottages. The Commission was given powers by a Royal Warrant of 1992 to survey, record, publish and maintain a database of ancient and historical sites, structures and landscapes in Wales. The records of the Commission had been amalgamated in 1964 with the Welsh section of the National Buildings Record of Wales to form the National Monuments Record of Wales, also based in Aberystwyth. This seeks to collect, maintain and make available a comprehensive record of the archaeological, architectural and historical monuments of Wales, and extensive collections of photographs, drawings, surveys and maps may be consulted at the library.

Cadw: Welsh Historic Monuments, established in 1984 with a statutory responsibility for protecting, conserving and presenting the ancient monuments and historic buildings of Wales, has published revised guides to Welsh historic sites. These are informative and attractively-illustrated publications, and recent examples include David M Robinson, *Neath Abbey* (2002), and A J Taylor, *Conway Castle and Town Walls* (5th ed. 2003). Regional guides include Sian Rees, *Dyfed* (1992), and Elizabeth Whittle, *Glamorgan and Gwent* (1992). Other publications which interpret the heritage of Wales include Elizabeth Whittle, *The Historic Gardens of Wales* (1992) and *Welsh Industrial Heritage: A Review*, ed. C Stephen Briggs

(1992) in CBA Research Report No. 79, comprising papers presented to the third Cadw Archaeological Conference, held at Cardiff in 1986.

Publishing ventures
Whilst a wide range of local and national and local institutions have facilitated and enhanced local historical studies in Wales, a number of publications illustrate the significant contributions of individuals. In this respect an outstanding contribution was made by Stewart Williams who was responsible for the *Glamorgan Historian* series, Vols I-XII (1963-81), together with several other publications on Glamorgan and volumes of photographs illustrating towns and districts in southeast Wales. Other recent publishing ventures which are examples of individual initiative include D B James's two volumes, *Myddfai: Its Land and Peoples* (1991) and *Ceredigion, Its Natural History*; and W R B Robinson, *Early Tudor Gwen, 1485-1547* (2002).

Reference has already been made to a number of English-language volumes which illustrate the immense contribution made by publishers in Wales to ensure an enhanced awareness of local history. Other examples of recent publications which focus on a specific subject or locality include M Senior, *Llandudno's Story* (Gwasg Carreg Gwalch, 1986); J B Sinclair and R W D Fenn, *Marching to Zion, Radnorshire Chapels* (Cadoc Books, 1990); *The Francis Jones Treasury of Historic Pembrokeshire*, ed. Caroline Charles-Jones, (Brawdy Books, 1998); Gwyn Briwnant-Jones and Denis Dunstone, *The Railways of Wales, circa 1900* (Gomer Press, 2000), Carol White and Sian Rhiannon Williams, *Struggle or starve: women's lives in the South Wales valleys between the two world wars* (Honno, 2002) and Gwynedd O Pierce, *Place-Names in Glamorgan* (Merton Priory Press, 2002). There is also an honourable tradition of Welsh-language publications in this field, and of especial significance in this respect are the *Cyfres y Cymoedd* ['Valleys' Series] published by Gwasg Gomer in ten volumes from 1993-2003 with each volume containing chapters on the cultural heritage of South Wales valley communities; and the volumes published by Gwasg Carreg Gwalch, in the *Cyfres Broydd Cymru* [Welsh Regions Series] featuring the various localities where national festivals, such as the National Eisteddfod, have been held.

On the other hand, other volumes relevant for the study of local history in Wales have been published in England. These include Ian Soulsby, *The Towns of Medieval Wales* (1983); M R C Price, *The Llanelly and Mynydd Mawr Railway* (1992); Michael A Roberts, *Researching Local History: The Human Journey* (1996) and Jim Roberts, *North Wales Transport* (1998) whilst E Hubbard, *Clwyd: Denbighshire and Flintshire* (2nd ed. 1994); and John Newman, *Glamorgan* (1995) and *Gwent* (2002) were published in 'The Buildings of Wales' series. The Chalford Publishing Company has also co-operated with Welsh record offices to publish volumes comprising collections of photographs of specific locations, in its *Archive Photographs Series*, and examples include *Cymoedd y Gwendraeth Valleys*, compiled by the

Economic Development and Leisure Department (Cultural Services), Carmarthenshire County Council (1997) and *Sir y Fflint, Flintshire*, compiled by Flintshire Record Office (1996).

BALH and other links

Welsh, as well as English local historians have benefited from the activities and publications of the British Association for Local History, and before its establishment, the Standing Conference for Local History, with both organisations seeking to encourage and assist the study of local history in Wales. The quarterly journal *The Local Historian* has published articles and book reviews of specific Welsh interest, including Brian Howells's article on 'Local history in Wales' in 1973 (Vol. 10 No. 8) and this author's report on the successful 'History in the Landscape' residential conference, held at Aberystwyth in 1994. This was organised by the BALH in association with the Department of Extra-Mural Studies, University of Wales Aberystwyth, the National Library of Wales, and the Ceredigion Antiquarian Society.

Other periodicals, which are not specifically concerned with Wales, but which contain relevant material and even occasionally articles which have a Welsh context include *The Agricultural History Review, Antiquity, The Archaeological Journal, Folk Life, History, The Historian, History Workshop Journal*, and *The Local Studies Librarian*. The first two issues, in 1997 and 1998, of *Tarmac Papers*, the series of annual volumes devoted to the archaeology and history of quarrying, contain studies respectively on quarries in Carmarthenshire and Anglesey.

Co-operative ventures

Welsh historians have also been involved in co-operative ventures, and regional chapters on Wales and the border shires have appeared in the 11 volumes of *The Agrarian History of England and Wales* published by the Cambridge University Press in the period 1967-2000. Information on the Welsh urban experience may be found in the three volumes of *The Cambridge Urban History of Britain* (2000). Several publications of the Oxford University Press also assist Welsh local historians, including R R Davies, *Lordship and Society in the March of Wales* (1978). A co-operative venture with the University of Wales Press has resulted in the appearance of four volumes in the proposed six-volume authoritative history of Wales, with volume VI, K O Morgan, *Rebirth of a Nation, Wales 1880-1980* published in 1981; and volumes II, III and IV in 1987, namely R R Davies, *Conquest, Coexistence and Change, Wales 1066-1485*; Glanmor Williams, *Recovery, Reorientation and Reformation, Wales c.1415-1642*; and G H Jenkins, *The Foundations of Modern Wales, Wales 1642-1780*. These volumes, together with John Davies's *A History of Wales*, published by the Penguin Press in 1993, provide a valuable national context to the work of those local historians whose activities reflect the vigour and energy which characterise historical studies in Wales today.

Further reading
Further information is available in the author's contribution on 'Welsh local and family history' in *The Oxford Companion to Local and Family History*, ed. David Hey (1996). Bibliographical data is provided in *A Bibliography of the History of Wales*, ed. Philip Henry Jones (microfiche, 1988); the National Library of Wales's *Llyfryddiaeth Cymru: Bibliography of Wales*, covering the period 1985-1994 in six volumes; and the online searchable databases for the catalogue of the National Library of Wales (www.llgc.org.uk) and the Archives Wales network (www.archivesnetworkwales.info). There is a select bibliography in *Settlement and Society in Wales*, ed. D Huw Owen (1989), a collection of essays considering various aspects of the development of the landscape, settlement patterns and social framework of Wales, and including Glanmor Williams's survey, 'Local and National History in Wales'.

Local History in the Republic of Ireland

James Scannell

Introduction
At the present time, local history is enjoying a great upsurge in interest throughout the island of Ireland and has become an important and popular activity both in Northern Ireland and the Republic of Ireland for a variety of reasons, with three organisations catering for the needs of local history societies:

i) The Federation of Ulster Local Studies (FULS) which covers Northern Ireland includes the three counties in the Republic of Ireland which form part of the geographical nine county province of Ulster and maintains links with the FOLHS in the Republic.

ii) The Border Counties History Collective (BCHC) which principally covers counties Cavan and Leitrim in the Republic of Ireland and county Fermanagh in Northern Ireland. This project also supports community groups engaged in employment schemes and local development groups.

iii) The Federation of Local History Societies (FOLHS) covers the Republic of Ireland and maintains links with the FULS in Northern Ireland.

The greatest growth and upsurge in local history interest in the Republic has taken place mainly over the past 20 years with events such as the celebration of Dublin's millennium in 1988, the 150th anniversary of the Famine in 1995, the bi-centenary of the 1798 rebellion, the millennium itself and more recently the bi-centenary of Robert Emmett's 1803 rising stimulating the formation of local history groups as communities research their local participation and links to these national events. Other events which have contributed to the formation of local history societies and groups include silver, golden, diamond and centenary anniversaries of churches, parishes, sporting clubs and voluntary organisations In rural areas, increased housing development and incomers has encouraged communities to record the history of the their respective areas before it is lost forever.

The situation prior to 1945
Prior to 1945, there were few local history societies in existence at either national or local level. Outside of the universities which had little interest in local history at that time, the only organisations collecting local history information were the Royal Irish Academy founded in 1785 by Lord Charlemont to 'advance the studies of science, polite literature and antiquities' and the Royal Society of Antiquaries, founded 1849, to 'preserve, examine and illustrate all Ancient Monuments and Memorials of the Arts, Manners and Customs of the past, as connected with the Antiquities, Language, Literature and History of Ireland'. Both were based in Dublin and still are. It was not until 1934 with the formation of the Old Dublin

Society that Dublin had its own specific local history society in the accepted sense. The Old Dublin Society was formed with the specific aim of promoting the study of the history and antiquity of Dublin and open to anyone interested in the study of Dublin in the widest sense. The Old Dublin Society now embraces County Dublin due to the rapid expansion of Dublin City and its incursion in the surrounding suburban areas, which started in the 1940s and is still on-going at the present time. Currently the Old Dublin Society holds weekly lectures during the winter and spring months and a series of monthly half day walking tours during the summer months. Papers read to the society at meetings and articles about Dublin and the Dublin area are published in the society's twice-yearly *Dublin Historical Record.*

The situation post-1945

World War Two, or Emergency as it is officially called in the Republic, brought a halt to a wide range of activities undertaken by many organisations due to transport restrictions and effects of rationing; but the Old Dublin Society managed to keep going. In 1941, the Maritime Institute of Ireland was established to 'promote greater awareness among the people of Ireland in the Sea, Shipping, Naval Service, Fisheries, Ports and Off Shore Resources' and currently undertakes an annual series of public lectures on Irish maritime history and maritime affairs. In the post Emergency years, two further national bodies catering for specific groups were formed: in 1946, the Irish Railway Record Society was established during a period of dramatic change to the Irish railway system following nationalisation in 1945. A group of railway enthusiasts wanted to preserve and record Ireland's railway history and currently the society fulfils these objectives through meetings and lectures. The *Journal of the Irish Railway Record Society* is published three times a year. The maintenance and operation of its extensive collection of material which is open to society members, researchers and members of the public is located in its headquarters in the former goods office in Dublin's Hueston Station (Kingsbridge). Uniquely, the Irish Railway Record Society has Cork area and London area branches, which hold their own lectures and events, and is perhaps the only Irish local history society to have an overseas branch.

The Military History Society of Ireland was formed in 1949 for the purpose of promoting the study of military history and, in particular, the history of warfare in Ireland and Irishmen at war. The society holds monthly lectures between October and April each year, in addition to annual outings, and publishes its journal *The Irish Sword* twice a year.

1963 saw the formation of another national body, the Railway Preservation Society of Ireland (RPSI), aimed at preserving various examples of Irish steam locomotives in working order and operating these on rail tours over the Irish mainline railway network in the Republic and Northern Ireland, which it currently does. In addition it publishes its annual journal *Five Foot Three*.

The 1970s and 1980s saw the evolution of many local history societies at community level due to increasing local development, resulting in the loss of local heritage and sense of place by existing inhabitants. This rise in local history interest and activity was marked by the formation of the Federation of Local History Societies (FOLHS) in 1981 to promote local history at local level on a national basis enabling local history societies to meet with each other to exchange experiences, news and publications. The influx of new comers into rural areas through urbanisation and housing developments and the celebration of Dublin's millennium in 1988 lead to the development of interest in local history in the greater Dublin area. The commemoration of the millennium led to the formation of some societies which are still active today.

In the 1990s, nationwide events to commemorate the 150th anniversary of the 1845 Famine and the bi-centenary of the 1798 rising led to a dramatic rise in the formation of local groups to explore and research activities within their respective communities during these periods of Irish history. Added to this was the pioneering work initiated by the National University of Ireland Maynooth (NUIM) during this decade which now offers specific courses in local history, based on the work of the UK's University of Leicester, adapted for Ireland, through MA and Certificate Courses in Local History for full-time and part-time students. The aim of NUIM is to raise the standard of local history research and writing at national level through the provision of courses and publication of research aids and continues to be the leader in this field. Other Irish third level institutions offering courses in local history are University College Cork (NUIC), University of Limerick (NUIL) and Queen's University, Belfast (QUB).

Presently, as more of the environment comes under threat from development, an increasing number of communities are forming local history societies or heritage groups to preserve and record the heritage and history of their past, using whatever means they have at their disposal.

How many societies?

It is hard to quantify precisely at the present time how many local history societies there are in the Republic of Ireland. During 2001, The Centre for Cross Border Studies (hereafter The Centre) based in Armagh, established in 1999 to research and develop co-operation across the Irish border in education health, business, public administration, communications and a range of other practical areas, undertook an all-Ireland local history survey. The Centre is a joint initiative by Queen's University Belfast, Dublin City University and the Workers for Peace and Reconciliation. The Centre asked a research team to undertake a local history society survey on an all-Ireland basis. This survey was carried out through research and questionnaires sent to all known history societies to provide the basis for the creation of the first all-Ireland register of local history societies including those affiliated to the FOLHS, the FULS, BCHS, and those with no affiliation to any of these. The research team from NUIM consisted of Dr. Jacinta Prunty, lecturer in the Department of Modern History, Dr Raymond Gillespie, Department of Modern History, NUIM, and Editor of the Maynooth Studies in Local History Studies series of publications, and Ms Maeve Mulryan Moloney MA, editor, at that time, of the *Local History Review* of the Federation of Local History Studies. The research team published their findings in *The Local History Project Co-operating North & South – A Report for the Centre for Cross Border Studies* (hereafter the Centre Report), in which 330 societies were identified throughout Ireland though it was stated that a comprehensive list would probably exceed 500 societies.

The Centre Report revealed the following number of local history societies on a per county basis throughout the Republic for 2001. These have been compared to the latest figures available extracted from the 2003 edition of *Local History Review* -

County	Centre Report 2001	Local History Review 2003	County	Centre Report 2001	Local History Review 2003
Carlow	2	2	Longford	1	1
Cavan	1	0	Louth	4	4
Clare	3	4	Mayo	3	3
Cork	16	17	Meath	6	6
Donegal	2	0	Monaghan	3	0
Dublin	19	21	Offaly	3	3
Galway	4	6	Roscommon	4	5
Kerry	2	2	Sligo	2	2
Kildare	7	8	Tipperary	9	10
Kilkenny	3	3	Waterford	1	1
Laois	3	4	Westmeath	3	3
Leitrim	1	1	Wexford	4	4
Limerick	7	7	Wicklow	6	9

Totals: Centre Report 2001 – 113 *Local History Review* 2003 – 126

I am aware that there are at least two societies in Co. Wicklow not listed in the Centre Report, and not members of the FOLHS, resulting in a revised 2003 figure for County Wicklow of 11 societies. Equally, the figure for Co. Dublin needs to be revised upwards by at least 6 societies to 27. Assuming that the figures for all the countries need to be revised slightly upwards, it is likely that there are between 150 and 250 local history societies in existence in the Republic.

Size

The largest local history societies by membership in the Republic are the Irish Railway Record Society, the Military History Society of Ireland, and the Royal Society of Antiquaries of Ireland, all of which have membership levels of 800+, closely followed by the Irish Traction Group and the County Donegal Railway Restoration Society (c. 500), the Old Dublin Society (c. 300), the Dun Laoghaire Borough Historical Society (c. 160) and the Rathmichael Historical Society (c. 120). Thereafter, membership of local history societies can range from as low as 5 members up to 100 with an average society membership figure lying somewhere in the region of between 35 – 50 members

Annual membership fees

The highest annual membership fees I have encountered for 2004 are £30 for the Irish Railway Record Society, £23 for the Royal Society of Antiquaries of Ireland, £18 for the Old Dublin Society and the Military History Society of Ireland, which includes mailing to members of copies of their respective journals, after which an amount of between £5 to £10 appears to be the norm.

With few exceptions, most local history societies are reluctant to revise annual membership fee levels on an annual or bi-annual basis due to the commonly held belief that a low annual membership fee will attract more members. Some societies do not increase their annual membership fee for several years for this reason and only do so when financial necessity requires it. The larger and more organised societies review their annual membership fee levels on an annual or bi-annual basis to reflect increasing overheads.

In an attempt to meet their expenses many societies levy members a meeting charge, with the national norm being in the region of £2.50. Most societies operate membership attendance records requiring members and visitors to record their attendance at meetings with these being scrutinised at intervals by their respective committees to see if any visitors are starting to attend on a regular basis with a view to asking them if they are interested in joining the society. Statistical analysis of these attendance records will reveal speakers and subjects which draw the greatest attendances and identify the regular attenders.

Frequency of activities

The local history programme year is generally September to May with some societies holding their annual long distance outings to places of historical interest during the June to August holiday period. Some societies do not hold a meeting in December while those that do hold meetings arrange their meeting night to fit with the Christmas period. Most societies meet on a monthly basis at a central location; a few meet bi-monthly, while the Old Dublin Society operates an autumn and spring 10 week series of lectures plus seven or eight half-day afternoon visits during the summer months to places of interest.

Location of meetings

Very few local history societies have their own premises in which to conduct meetings and activities. The Royal Society of Antiquaries of Ireland, and the Irish Railway Record Society are some of the few organisations which have their own premises. The remainder of the societies hold their meetings in a diverse range of locations such as school halls, university or college lectures rooms, church halls, parish and community centres, hotel rooms and public house function rooms with no guarantee of tenure. It is not unusual for a local history society to move meeting place from time to time for a variety of reasons, which include cost or their room being assigned to other organisations.

The cost of hiring meeting rooms varies, depending on location and the charges for the accommodation and can vary from as low as £10 to as high as £50 per meeting. It is usually the main item of expenditure shown in annual financial accounts. A few societies that meet in hotel rooms or public houses receive the use of rooms free of charge in the expectation that members and visitors will avail themselves of the facilities therein!

Meeting night

Tuesdays, Wednesdays and Thursdays are generally the most popular meeting nights. No meetings take place on Saturday or Sundays though some societies hold half-day outings on these days in the form of walks or visits to places of interest at various times during the year, usually during the summer months.

Meeting time and duration

In general, most local history societies start between 7.30 and 8.30 p.m. 8 p.m. is the most popular time. Meetings are usually of two hours duration with the guest speaker expected to speak for between forty-five to sixty minutes followed by thirty minutes discussion. Sometimes refreshments are provided. A few societies hold a short talk before the main lecture.

Meeting attendance

Most local history societies are open to members of other local history societies and to the public. One or two societies still restrict attendance at their meetings to 'Members only or Members and their Guests only' which is a somewhat self-defeating policy as it denies these societies a valuable means of obtaining new members. While this policy may be justified on the grounds of controlling access to a meeting place due to security requirement, insurance or other reasons, the majority of societies welcome visitors to their meetings to boost income and membership.

Attendance levels at lectures vary from society to society depending on the choice of night, subject, speaker, weather conditions, and any other competing local events or television programmes taking place that night or breaking live news stories. The average meeting attendance ranges between thirty-five and fifty.

Committee membership profile

In general terms, most local history societies are finding it increasingly hard to recruit new committee members as there appears to be reluctance by many members to go forward for committee posts at AGMs. Reasons given include lack of time, not considering themselves capable of doing this work or a reluctance to get involved. Many memberships are happy to have everything organised for them by their elected committees but not to get involved in the running of their respective societies or to undertake some of this work themselves. Increasingly, AGMs of many societies have become the one night when there is a very low turnout of members with many staying away so that they can't be nominated for a committee post or be called upon to undertake some work for the society. More and more AGMs have become brief affairs with the reports of the out-going committee being placed before members for discussion and adoption followed by the election for committee positions – in many cases the out-going committee is returned unopposed. Vacancies arising from to the retirement of officers may have to be filled by co-option, or undertaken by existing committee members, or left vacant.

Many societies are now including a lecture or short talk immediately preceding the AGM in an effort to encourage attendance. While many societies have rules specifying how long an individual post-holder may serve, in many cases these rules have had to be suspended in order to enable the existing post-holders to carry on in the absence of new candidates. In some societies, members regularly return the same committee year after year on the basis that they don't want to break up a winning team with new post-holders joining only when an existing post-holder retires or makes it known that they are not prepared to continue. This lack of interest by members means that in some societies, the same committee is returned year in and year out with vacant committee positions due to resignations or retirements only being filled by co-option. A few societies exist in name only and have gone into suspension because of the refusal of the existing committee to remain in office and the refusal of members to stand for election. In general, the age range of committee members tends to be range of 55 upwards.

Sustainability of societies

Concern has to be expressed about a number of societies which may cease to exist because they are being operated by a small number of committed individuals. In the South Dublin area, which has the highest concentration of local history societies in close proximity of each other in the Republic, there are at least four societies being operated in this manner. Three of them will most likely cease to function unless someone with enthusiasm comes forward to keep them going while the fourth will probably merge with a nearby society.

Age profile of members

In general, the age profile of local history society members tends to be in the 45–70 year age group; the tendency is for very few young people to join local history societies. In their forties they often become interested in researching their family or some aspect of the locality they work or live in. While many local history studies are part of the second level history syllabus in schools, students tend not be to become interested in this subject again until later in life. While many local history societies visit schools and give presentations on various aspects of local history, very few students join at this point as their priority is studying for the Leaving Certificate Examination (A and O Levels), the results of which are used for third level entry purposes through the Central Application Office process. Members under 40 tend to be the exception rather than the rule in most history societies.

Speakers and lecturers

It is virtually impossible for local history societies to produce an annual programme of talks covering their immediate locality. While this may be possible for the first or second year of operation, generally, after that it is necessary to augment the programme with some wider local history subjects dealing with events in another community or at national level which ideally have a local link or connection.

While there is a small pool of local amateur or professional historians prepared to present talks to societies on an on-going basis, it is usually left to individual programme secretaries to try and locate speakers who will be prepared to address meetings, whether they are authors of recently published books, local historians, researchers or third level institution lecturers .

The Centre Report made the following recommendations on this topic:
- A panel of lecturers, stating their topic(s) should be made available in each region of Ireland either through the Federations or the County Libraries.
- Lecturers should be invited on a cross-border basis.
- Local history societies should pool their resources to invite lecturers.
- Lecturers should be booked at least six months in advance.
- Local newspapers, local radio and the internet should be used to publicise forthcoming lectures .
- More flexible timetables for lecturers, to bring in a wider audience.

Unfortunately, most of the above has not yet come to pass. County library local history services vary due in part to funding and the availability of resources. Some new libraries or existing ones which have been refurbished or upgraded have state of the art facilities, excellent archives and trained staff to assist inquirers and have a policy of collecting local history information on an on-going basis. While much local history information is available in various county library headquarters, those living some distance away often find it difficult to access it. At individual branch level, the quantity of local history material held varies as often the branch collection of this material relates only to the area served; the collection of this material is down to the enthusiasm and interest of individual librarians and the resources available.

There is no national database of individuals prepared to address local history societies that societies or country libraries can access. At the present time, the FOLHS has not compiled a database of this information but hopes to include it in future issues of the *Local History Review*, which planned from 2004 to publish details of individuals prepared to present talks to local history societies. Country libraries may use this information to answer inquiries and while individual country libraries may have their have their own databases of speakers, there is no central body from which this information can be accessed.

Excluding the Dublin area, the distances between local history societies often makes joint meetings difficult to organise and impractical to operate. Within the Dublin area, members of the many various societies are able to attend each other's lectures on an individual basis and it not uncommon for an individual to hold membership of more than one local history society although joint society meetings are the exception rather than the rule.

The national press devotes very little coverage to local history activities and despite attempts to interest editors in running a weekly local history column in the major daily national morning newspapers which elicited some interest, editors cited lack of space as the reasons why they cannot accommodate such a column. The same applies to the Sunday papers. Coverage in local newspapers varies from title to title with local history society coverage depending on the editorial interest in this topic. While meetings may be advertised in 'What's On'-type columns, post meeting coverage will depend on reports submitted by PROs or District Correspondents and the amount of space available. Several local newspapers which run 'Looking Back', 'Times Past', 'Remember When' - type features, usually written by local historians, have proved to be very popular with readers.

One newspaper, which has consistently publicised local history societies meetings in the South Dublin Area for over 12 years, has been the weekly *SouthSide People (East)*, currently called *SouthSide People*, through the publication of a dedicated 'Local History Events' column covering the activities of the 16-20 local history societies active within its readership area. This newspaper has been able to do this due to the dedication of a voluntary contributor who compiles this column on a weekly basis and the excellent support for it given by the editor.

Two national quarterly publications *Archaeology Ireland* and *History Ireland* also carry 'What's On' listings but in general only those societies which have prepared long-term fixed programmes are featured in these magazines because of the editorial requirement that this information should be submitted well in advance of publication.

Local radio, which will usually broadcast notices free of charge, is used by some local history societies to publicise their meetings. In the Dublin area, where there are several community radio stations, a number of them broadcast specific local history programmes on a weekly basis such as *Looking Back* on Anna Livia FM, *History On Your Doorstep* on Dublin South Community Radio, *Living History* on NEAR FM, *The Moira Byrne Programme* on East Coast Radio. Each of these stations receive a weekly script known as *Event Diary* written by the compiler of the *SouthSide People* column tailored specifically to the requirements of each of these radio stations. A copy of the script is also submitted to national broadcaster Lyric FM for the daily *Lyric Notes* 'What's On' feature.

The internet is slowly being used by more and more societies to publicise their meetings and publications. Some websites are basic, others are quite comprehensive with the quality, accuracy, and currency of information displayed on these websites varying from local history society to local history society depending on their respective webmasters.

Publications

The majority of local history societies, which publish journals usually do so on an annual basis, generally in an A5 64-page format. The Irish Traction Group's *The Irish Mail* and The Genealogical Society of Ireland's *GSI Journal* are published four times a year; The Irish Railway Record Society's *Journal of the Irish Railway Record Society* is published three times a year; the Military Society of Ireland's *The Irish Sword* is published twice a year as are the Old Dublin Society's *Dublin Historical Record* which uniquely runs to 130 pages per issue. The County Donegal Railway Restoration Society's *The Phoenix*, the Medal Society of Ireland's *Journal of the Medal Society of Ireland*, the Arklow Historical Society, Ballinteer Family History Society, County Wicklow Genealogical Society, Dun Laoghaire Borough Historical Society, the Roundwood and District Folklore and Historical Society, and the Wicklow Historical Society, are some of the societies which produce an annual publication.

Most publications are made available to members as part of the annual membership subscription with many surplus copies being sold at meetings of their respective societies with some copies being sold locally through newsagents and bookshops. There is reluctance by many local history societies to provide copies for sale through major booksellers due to their commercial sales commission charge of between 33% to 50% of the cover price, which makes it uneconomic for many societies to sell publications in this manner.

Currently, there is no national database of local history publications produced or available that inquirers can access despite the best efforts of the FOLHS. For a number of years, the FOLHS has been trying to build up its own library of local history publications through copies donated to it from member societies which are also invited to list their available publications in the FOLH *Local History Review*, but regrettably not all local history societies submit annual activity reports to it, nor does it include information on societies which are not affiliated to it.

The Centre Report commented that while local history societies have an ever-increasing output of journals, newsletters and books, some of which are produced to a very high standard, there was ample scope for improvement in the research and presentation of these publications, including some produced by the smaller societies. The Centre Report also identified the urgent need to establish minimum scholarly standards for the production of journals and monographs, particularly where they are publicly funded. This was a reference to the fact that articles in many journals do not contain footnotes or reference sources. Some editors exclude this information on the basis that the space saved can be used to include other articles. There can be no doubt that guidelines for publications to establish a minimum national standard should be produced and available for the guidance of editors and contributors.

Price-wise, local history society publications sell from as low as £3 to as high as £15 - the average selling price is somewhere is the region of £5 - £7.

Some societies in rural and large urban centres rely on sponsorship or advertising to meet the costs of producing publications. Token grants may be awarded to local history societies by local authorities under the Arts Acts to assist publication but usually will not exceed £250 unless an exceptional publication is intended and even here there are financial limits on how much of the overcall cost will be grant-aided.

Authors of books on local history are finding it increasingly difficult to obtain funding to get their works published as there is no central body to provide funding. While the Heritage Council of Ireland does grant aid to some publications, in the main these are from established authors or on subjects that have national interest.

Funding

Despite widespread recognition of the importance of local history, very little financial support is given to appropriate societies from central government or by local authorities. Even the FOLHS receives no central government or local authority funding towards the vital work it does but has to rely on income from membership subscriptions and affiliation fees.

Arts Acts funding tends to be restrictive due to the legislative criteria under which grants are awarded and to the fact that local history societies have to compete with other organisations for the limited sums made available by local authorities. A qualifying society usually receives a grant of up to £60 towards the cost of a special lecture. Local history societies receive no contribution from local authorities to cover their annual operating costs. A grant of up to £200 may be provided towards the costs of a publication. This amount may be increased if a publication is being produced in association with a local authority or county library service. The level of grants will also vary from local authority to local authority depending on the financial resources available and the number of qualifying applicants.

The four items of highest expenditure incurred by most local history societies are:
- Meeting rent
- Public liability insurance
- Speakers' fees
- Postage and stationery

The FOLHS has always been acutely aware of the high cost of public liability insurance and provides a fixed cost public liability scheme with a leading Irish insurance broker which is available only to affiliated societies.

The Federation of Local History Societies

The FOLHS, a voluntary body with no central office, is the national organisation representing and promoting local history and the activities of local history societies in the Republic. In common with many other voluntary organisations all mail is directed to the private homes and workplaces of committee members, and operates without any form of state or local authority aid, having to rely on affiliated societies to fund its activities. The FOLHS was formed in 1981 to encourage research in the fields of history, archaeology, folk-life and folklore, the exchange of information between affiliated societies through the medium of newsletters, publications, seminars etc., the development of mutual support between affiliated societies and to encourage the publication of information of historical interest and the better utilisation of archives.

The FOLHS holds an annual spring seminar and its AGM in the autumn, with both these events being hosted by designated local history societies which usually provide a local input to these events by way of talks and a walking tour of their locality in the afternoon. Each member society is invited to send two representatives to these events to report back to their respective societies. The FOLHS also publishes an annual directory, *Local History Review*, which contains activity reports from affiliated societies, details of their publications, articles on local history and a contact name and address for every FOLHS society. Each affiliated society receives two copies of this publication which is also available for purchase by individuals. Occasional newsletters are also sent to affiliated societies.

The FOLHS has published a number of booklets with guidance and advice on setting up local history societies, on their operation and on the establishment and operation of voluntary/civic museums.

While the FOLHS has contacts with the FULHS and holds events in partnership with it, as yet the FOLHS has no formal contact with the British Association for Local History (BALH). I am currently providing the BALH with information on a monthly basis on local history activities in the Republic pending the formal establishment of contacts between the FOLHS and the BALHS.

Not all local history societies in the Republic are members of the FOLHS perhaps not knowing of its existence, feeling that it has nothing to offer them or simply not being interested in joining it due to the parochial nature of local history.

The Dublin area

The Dublin area is unique in that it has the highest concentration of local history societies in the Republic which work in conjunction with each other. In addition national history societies to which reference has been made earlier in this article, are based in Dublin.

The Federation of Local History Societies (FOLHS) includes twenty-one societies, but the total number of local history societies is likely to be between twenty-seven and thirty-five when non-FOHLS members are included.

In South Dublin, most of the local history societies are members of the Barony of Rathdown Network of Local History Societies (BORN) an informal forum for representatives from local history societies to meet twice a year and which tries to implement the aims of the FOLHS at grass roots level by assisting in advice and guidance. On Dublin's north side, the Association of Final Societies undertakes a similar role to BORN with a similar network of local history societies operating in Co. Kildare. Hopefully, at some time we could yet see again, as in the past, support from Dublin City Council to mount local history exhibitions.

Conclusion

Overall, as the formation of new societies and the involvement of libraries – such as Dublin City Library and Archive, Pearce Street, Wicklow Country Library, Fingal County Council Library, Tallaght and Wexford County Library Service shows, interest in local history is alive and well in the Republic. The FOLHS, in association with third level institutions, can play a major role in further developments although this will entail a full-time staff of two or three persons to assist local societies in their efforts and an annual income of around £150,000, which is not likely to be available from central or local government in the near future.

Sources

Publications
S J Connolly, Editor, *The Oxford Companion to Irish History*, Oxford, 1999.
Frank Taaffe, Editor, *Local History Review No 12. - 2003*, Athy, 2003.
Jacinta Prunty, Raymond Gillespie, Maeve Mulryan-Moloney, *The Local History Project – Co-operating North and South: A Report for the Centre for Cross Border Studies*, Oct. 2002.
D J Hickey & J E Doherty, *A New Dictionary of Irish History from 1800*, Dublin 2003.
Maeve Mulryan-Moloney, Editor, *Local History Review No. 11 – 2002*, Naas, 2002.

Programmes and Leaflets
The County Donegal Railway Restoration Society
The Irish Railway Record Society
The Irish Traction Group
The Maritime Institute of Ireland
The Military History Society of Ireland
The Railway Preservation Society of Ireland
The Royal Society of Antiquaries of Ireland

Interviewees
Robert Butler, Co.Wicklow Library Service
Henry Cairns, Trustee, Old Bray Society
John Callan, Enniskerry History Society
Liam Clare, Foxrock Local History Club
Joe Lawlor, Mount Merrion Historical Society
Philip Lecane, The Royal Dublin Fusiliers Association
John Lennon, Dundrum and District History Society
Michael Kelliher Bray Public Library
Tom Moran, Ballybrack-Killiney Local History Society
Ms Eileen Murray, Retired Chief Librarian, Bray Public Library
Ms Darine Nuttall, Kilmacanogue History Society
Redmond O'Hanlon, Rathmichael Historical Society
Jim Rees, Local Historian, Arklow, Co.Wicklow
Chris Ryan, Administrator, Ballinteer Family History Society
James Scannell, Administrator, Barony of Rathdown Network, PRO Old Dublin Society, PRO Rathmichael Historical Society, PRO Bray Cualann Historical Society
Colin Scudds, Hon. Secretary, Dun Laoghaire Borough Society
Ms Aileen Shortt, Greystones Archaeological and Historical Society
Peter Supple, Kilmacud Stillorgan Local History Society
Brian White, Hon. Secretary, Bray Cualann Historical Society.

THE SOCIALIST HISTORY SOCIETY

The Socialist History Society was founded in 1992 and includes many leading Socialist and labour historians, both academic and amateur, in Britain and overseas. The SHS holds regular events, public meetings and one-off conferences, and contributes to current historical debates and controversies. The society produces a range of publications, including the journal *Socialist History*. We can sometimes assist with individual student research.

The SHS is the successor to the Communist Party History Group, established in 1946. The society is now independent of all political parties and groups. We are engaged in and seek to encourage historical studies from a Marxist and broadly-defined left perspective. We are concerned with every aspect of human history from early social formations to the present day and aim for a global reach.

We are particularly interested in the struggles of labour, women, progressive and peace movements throughout the world, as well as the movements and achievements of colonial peoples, black people, and other oppressed communities seeking justice, human dignity and liberation.

Each year we produce two issues of our journal *Socialist History*, one or two historical pamphlets in our *Occasional Papers* series, and members' newsletters. We hold a public lecture and debate in London five times per year. In addition, we organise occasional conferences, book-launch meetings, and joint events with other sympathetic groups.

Join the Socialist History Society!
Members receive all our serial publications for the year at no extra cost and regular mailings about our activities. Members can vote at our AGM and seek election to positions on the committee, and are encouraged to participate in other society activities.

Annual membership fees (renewable every January):
Full UK £20.00
Concessionary UK £14.00
Overseas full £25.00
Overseas concessionary £19.00
For details of institutional subscriptions, please e-mail the treasurer on francis@socialisthistorysociety.co.uk .

To join, please send your name and address plus a cheque/PO payable to **Socialist History Society** to: SHS, 50 Elmfield Road, Balham, London SW17 8AL.

Visit our websites on www.socialisthistorysociety.co.uk and www.socialist-history-journal.org.uk .